GO

MOMSHIE

MOTHERHOOD

KEEP IT REAL

GET IT DONE

VICTORIA DANG

PRAISE FOR GO MOMSHIE

"Go Momshie is a wonderful testament to new moms. I wish I had this book 18 years ago when I had my first child. Victoria weaves in some practical guides to enhance your motherhood experience. Along with these tips, Victoria reminds us that perspective and a clear mindset paves the way to a happy, healthy family dynamic and relationship between mothers and their babies. Go Momshie is a must read and is definitely a book that has some little hidden secrets that will surely brighten up your day."

Pashmina P.
International bestselling author of
"The Cappuccino Chronicles Trilogy" and
"What is a Gupsey?"
Founder and CEO, The Online Author's Office
M.Ed. International Teaching

"As a mom to my beautiful daughter, Maya, I know what a special role motherhood is, especially for first time moms. In her book, Victoria guides us to following our intuition through a step by step process with helpful practices, anecdotes and valuable tips to make it easier to get through our toughest days. This book is a must read! A companion and a legacy piece for mothers across the globe."

Natalie Glebova
Miss Universe 2005, Author "I AM WINNING",
Self-love & Mindfulness Coach

"I love Victoria's Go Momshie blogs and now this book! Go Momshie offers a whole new perspective for moms. There's been a huge awakening on how parenting is now, compared to generations ago. Go Momshie opens your eyes to decoding parenthood, while giving the reader updated solutions. This is a must read for mothers, wives and, most importantly, women who care for themselves."

Charm Fernandez
President and CEO Sophistechated Marketing &
Developments Inc. Alberta, Canada

GO MOMSHIE
Copyright © 2021 Victoria Dang

Permission should be addressed in writing to Victoria Dang at gomomshie@gmail.com

Editor | Cover Design | Layout
Online Author's Office

Paperback: 978-1-7373897-0-5
LCCN: 978-1-7373897-0-5

DEDICATION

This book is dedicated to all the loving Momshies out there and to my Seiya, who keeps me on my toes. Thank you for teaching me how to be the best Momshie ever!

I also dedicate this book to all of the survivors of COVID-19. This disease emerged like a monster on a global scale in 2020. Whilst writing this book, Seiya and I contracted the virus and were in quarantine for two weeks. I can't begin to describe how painful the ordeal was, and how much I suffered with an excruciating headache and a fever of 38.8 degrees for days. My eyes swelled up and became bloodshot, and I felt like my head was going to roll off my body. It was here in this space that I was moved to understand that resilience, strength and looking after another human being, whilst infected, had changed me. I am the Momshie I am today because I got through it with the love and support of my family, who I would also like to dedicate this book to.

Thank you to everyone who came to my rescue — my husband Ryu, my mom, my sisters and my mentors, who stood by my side even when I couldn't open my eyes to read the edits from my editor. It is through these people that I wear a badge of pride and honor in knowing that good people indeed make the world go round. As this virus leaves my body and vanishes into the air, I say with confidence that there is so much more to learn, and I know that education in many forms helps to beat the ignorance out of us all.

A life worth saving is a life worth giving. Be strong, Momshies. This world is made for us.

ACKNOWLEDGEMENTS

First of all, I would like to thank my baby, Seiya, for inspiring me to write this book. He may not be able to read it right now, since he's too young, but I hope that he'll hold this book in his hands in the future with a smile on his face and with a proud heart.

This book would never be possible if it wasn't for my supportive husband, Ryu. He has been there to cheer me up, especially during those moments when I doubted myself and was feeling discouraged. It was a great relief and comfort to know that he managed our household so I could complete my writing. From the bottom of my heart, I would also like to thank Ryu for letting me explore and discover what I want to achieve in life. Thank you for your respect of my heart's desires and for endlessly pushing me to do something else outside motherhood. I'm proud to say to everyone that I have the perfect man right here. I love you, Baboo! Thank you for making parenting fun and manageable.

I also would like to acknowledge my mom. She has been an inspiration and a big influence in my life. She regaled me with Momshie stories and reminded me how she did it back in the day when she was raising us, her four children. Her pride in me for writing this book is a reward unto itself. Thank you, Mommy, for loving me and caring for me.

I would like to thank my siblings — Abigail, Lester and Alfredo. Thank you for cheering for me and for mocking me to push me even harder. Your jokes and your support really helped me a lot. For the rest of the Castilla, Balbaguio and Dang families, who have believed in my ability to write this book and share and inspire other Momshies around the world, thank you.

I also would like to thank Ms. Pash, my mentor, my friend and my former work colleague, for reaching out to me and for opening up an opportunity to start off my literary journey. Her trust and her words fueled my passion in writing. It's all because of her and the OAO team that my book has started to come to fruition. Thank you for reading every word a thousand times and making sure that I stayed true to my craft and intention.

To the Go Momshie Support Group, friends and other Momshies out there! Thank you for fixing my crown; for letting me feel that I'm not alone on this journey. Your support and your messages really helped me to keep moving forward in writing this book.

Finally, thank you Lord for your wisdom and guidance.

CONTENTS

INTRODUCTION

Shit Really Does Happen!

There I was, one fine day, lounging on the sofa as I usually do, watching TV while enjoying my husband's company. Almost as if a shadow had crept up behind us, a foul smell percolated up my nose and pierced my nostrils until I was trapped and suffocated by the stench. I ignored it for a couple of minutes until my sensitive nose could no longer endure the attack on my senses. I pulled my head around to reach under my arm to smell my armpit. Nope! This wasn't it. I checked my breath. Nope! That wasn't it either. And then I felt it; a sticky soft mucous substance touched my lap. I looked down and saw my three-month-old son's face smiling at me, and a look of relief was on his face like he had accomplished something grand. It was then that I realized he had pooped all over my leg. Aha! The culprit had been found!

I held him high, away from me, and tried to put him somewhere other than my lap, but the poop just fell onto the floor as if to mark his territory. I looked at myself; my shirt, my pants, my hands, my legs, the floor, the couch, the carpet — all covered with poop! I just wanted to break down and cry. How could such a small little human make such a big mess? This was when I realized that my whole life was actually turned upside down, inside out and round and round when I had my baby. And just like the mess he made all over the place, he had shown me that he had forever marked my world. I was not destined to clean up after him all the time, but in that instant, I knew that my son's reliance on me was showing me that he needed me, and I was the one who would have to protect him, save him and CLEAN him when he was dirty. It suddenly dawned on me that my life was full of responsibilities, which I never knew existed before I had the love of my life, Seiya. Nevertheless, that day, with poop all over the place, including on me, I felt like, "SHIT!!! This is way too much!"

Seiya, I hope when you are reading this to your own kids, you will know how much you really did actually make me smile, through every up and down we have been through!

CHAPTER 1

The Weight of it All Gets to us

"*I'm too tired to even take a shower*", I said to myself as I laid on my bed staring at the ceiling. My eyes were cracked wide open, but my body was so stiff. I couldn't count how many times I told myself, "*I feel like my body is dying*".

That night I felt so exhausted, and I looked over to my side. There was my husband, happily browsing on his phone. I turned to him and said, "You know what, I feel like I'm dying, literally. I just feel that my body is going to give up. If that happens, please take care of Seiya."

I meant what I said because the pressure of everything around me felt like it was caving in on me. My husband paused and I got a loving pat on the head. He wanted to give me some kind of reality check as tears started to stream down my face. He turned to hug me and said, like a father would say to a child, "No one is dying! Stop saying that word."

What I'm saying, Momshies, is that nobody's really dying here; it's just me, or us, feeling like we are helpless, tired and maybe sometimes unappreciated.

That big, loving pat on the head woke me up to a reality that being tired is okay, but feeling like I need to 'lie down to rest and not wake up' is not okay. I have witnessed some moms feeling and looking so tired, yet they keep on going. On these days, Momshies, we must realize when to stop and take a deep breath, especially when the weight of it gets to us. We must do something about it. It can become dangerous if you ignore this feeling. I am very lucky to have a supportive partner in my life, but some of us are single, and I want you to know, right now, right here, that you are never alone. If you ever need a helping hand, or someone to listen or just someone to have a laugh with, know that I am here for you. In writing this book, I hope that you will find a friend in me, and you will find support in the pages of this writing to help you get through some hard days. Believe me, there are some days where you just feel like you want to crawl into a ball and disappear.

So how can we possibly deal with ourselves when we're overly exhausted?

YOU HAVE TO DO YOU!

You know yourself better than anybody else; you know your limits, strengths and weaknesses. There might be times when you don't understand yourself, especially when you're getting through the stage of shock due to the changes happening around you, like being a first-time mom.

Transitioning to the role of a mom for the first time is a completely shocking experience and undeniably overwhelming. It's like driving a car for the first time. It takes time and practice to gain endurance and rhythm to get used to it and, most of all, having the confidence to embark on something totally unknown and new. Believe me, I have confidence. I love to dance, and in my previous careers I have always been in customer service roles, so I know about confidence. Yet, when Seiya was born, some parts of me became frightened, overwhelmed, and my confidence plummeted. All because I was now in charge of another human life besides my own.

Being YOU as a mom will definitely take away so much baggage from your past, as you are NOT living with the expectations of other people, for example, your in-laws, parents, friends or the online community.

Being yourself means just doing only what you can for the time being. This does not mean doing the minimum, Momshies. It means that you do things at your own time and pace. You may start slow on this motherhood journey. So what? It's YOU. You will grow and adjust at your own pace and excel in some areas you didn't know you could until you dive into discovery. You will sometimes feel like you are being pushed into the unknown, and that's okay because with discovery comes adventure. Motherhood, after all, is a very poignant time of absolute revelation. Think of it as going on a whole new contingency, to a whole new world!

When you decide to carve out time for yourself and exercise self-care, you will realize that things will never feel like they are 'too much'. Everyone is unique and has their own way of dealing with things. Embrace your authenticity and grow while learning with your child at your pace. Stop comparing yourselves to others, Momshies. It's not worth it! A good and practical example is breastfeeding. A lot of Momshies out there are showing off their breast milk stash, especially online. This could be seen as good inspiration for others, yes. But it also adds pressure on other Momshies who are struggling.

Let me remind you that you are not supposed to have plenty of milk from day one. If you do have an endless supply right from the start, then more power to you. If you don't have too much to show off then that's okay too. Putting pressure on yourself for no reason is a waste of time and doesn't give you enough time to focus on other things. Be grateful that your baby has options, and so do you. There is nothing wrong with formula. Moreover, if you want to exclusively breastfeed, great; but if you feel you need some time-off, don't be afraid to let yourself go and rest. You need it too.

Each mother has a unique parenting style. It's okay not to be the same as other moms. It's your lifestyle, your way. Motherhood is not a competition; there's no cash prize for those who can breastfeed for two years or for those who can't do it all.

As a young mother, I have come across a few Momshies who have revealed to me their experiences after they started living the lifestyle that works for them and their family. I will share a couple of these with you below.

Testimonials

"That is how we do it back in the day...",

"You shouldn't give this or that to your child...",

" You should do this, do that..." etc. This is just some of the advice I have heard since I had my baby. I appreciate them, but I firmly believe that parenting is not a 'one size fits all' kind of thing. It gives me joy to be able to raise my daughter the way I want to. I get to tailor my parenting style to her needs. It doesn't only give me the chance to know her more and build a good bond with her, but I also get to discover who I am as a parent. The takeaway is that I become a better person too. Kids tend to mimic their parents, so building their character starts from home. This is why I make sure that I provide a positive, safe and loving environment for my child, so she can acquire the best qualities we have and share it with the world."

—Onana Hancock, a first-time mom

"When my kid was still a baby, I remember feeling offended when relatives would sometimes try to take control of my own process as a mom. They have different opinions about single moms like me. Being able to care for someone and love your family the way that you want to love them is really a gift. I am beyond happy to make decisions for me and my kid out of a great relationship that I built with him as his mom. Even when I am far away from him, I know

how to be his mom, and I really couldn't care less about other people's opinion unless I ask for them. Right now, I have created an inner circle for me and my kid, and for us it works. I feel like it's the best way to be at peace with myself and my role as a mom."

—Danice Margret De Leon, a single mom

DON'T HESITATE TO ASK FOR HELP

Whoever says that you're weak when you ask for help does not belong in your world, your tribe, your space, and they are not worthy of your time. Help is always around the corner. And I am here to listen, so if you really can't find anyone to reach out to, please email me.

When you're taking care of your only child but it really feels like you're taking care of three babies, it's a sign, Momshies, that you need some assistance. You cannot take care of your baby if you don't look after yourself. Your baby will be able to feel your exhaustion if you don't take time out to do something for yourself every single day.

YES it's true	★ *Motherhood is challenging.* ★ *Moms face unique battles every day.* ★ *It's a long and never-ending job.*
What is NOT true	★ *Moms need to do it alone.* ★ *Mom gets more credit if she manages to do everything by herself.* ★ *Mom's focus should be her child and husband only. Her world must only revolve around her family.* ★ *Moms need to endure the pain, the exhaustion and get used to it.* ★ *Moms should be more patient because that's just how it is.* ★ *Moms should be an expert at everything.*

If I were you, I would throw away all these false assumptions into the garbage, and start living and owning your true and authentic notion of what you think motherhood is and should be. Coming together with people in your community who have like-minded ideas is a good way to indirectly ask for help.

Suggestions for Some Practical Ways to Ask for Help

Maximize the love of your in-laws, parents or close family friends, who innately have love for your child

Drop your baby off with them for an hour or two, and get in some time for a nap or time for yourself. Believe me, it sounds like a quick fix, but it will help a lot. Leaving your child with a very trusted family or friend will garner peace of mind, and this will help you to get adequate rest with less worry. Furthermore, giving your parents or in-laws time with your little one can bring them so much joy and memories that are so precious.

Maximize the presence of your siblings, relatives and friends. Sometimes, they will have more energy than you to play with your little one. Once they visit, let your baby bond and play with them. It's also an opportunity for you to get a breather and have some down time. Rejuvenation is the key to a happy and healthy Momshie, and you will be able to deliver more. Running on empty will cause a lot of frustration not only for you and your baby, but for everyone else around you too.

If you have enough savings or extra money to hire a *yaya* or a nanny, then do it!

Some people are against yayas or nannies, especially when you hear and believe some of the horror stories that have happened to some families. Don't fret; instead learn how to be aware of your nanny's credentials through the screening process. If you're a working mom and your family is not around or available, then a nanny is a notion you might have to consider. But even if you're not working, if you have saved some money for a nanny, it's going to be a big help for you, Momshie.

So once you have made the decision to employ a nanny, set up a thorough structure for recruitment, and establish a proper system to be followed when they are taking care of your baby. That way, you're still in control and aware of what's going on with your baby even when you're at work.

To be more specific and practical when hiring a nanny, here are some tips to consider during the **recruitment phase:**

a. You may find posts on different social platforms, but always ask them to send their resumes via email.

b. The first task of hiring a potential nanny is your request to send their CV or resume to your email, as stated above. With this simple task, you can already filter out those who can follow instructions and those who cannot. Also, when your nanny shows that they know how to send an email, you can relax knowing she can always get in touch with you when you are working. This is so important for when there is an emergency with your baby; her knowledge and common sense is a sure indication that she will know when to call you if there is indeed an emergency.

c. Set up a video call and ask personal questions about her family, like if she has children of her own. This will enable you to gauge whether or not she has some maternal instincts. It is paramount to ask about previous work experience. This might sound like common sense, but you want to hire someone who knows how to handle a baby with patience, empathy and compassion. Ask everything about her qualifications, and evaluate how she handles situations by asking her some questions about baby's bath time, playtime, nap time etc. You may also verify her experiences by calling her personal references or studying details that can be found on her resume.

d. Make sure to hire somebody who does not have a baby or toddler at home. It is better to hire a nanny who has children who are in high school or college, or even working. That way, your nanny will focus on your baby when she is at work and give undivided attention to your baby's needs while she is on duty. We all know, as working moms, that when we have a baby at home, we are constantly thinking about them and worrying about their safety and well-being. We need to know that our baby is someone else's top priority when we aren't with them.

e. When you have ticked all the boxes and you are happy with your nanny's expertise, prepare an employment contract (very important) and set a probation period so you can make sure your professional relationship is a compatible one. Yours and her energy, coupled with working together, has to be in alignment.

HERE ARE SOME TIPS FOR WHEN YOUR NANNY IS ON-THE-JOB

a. On the first day, make sure to lay out everything the nanny needs to do. You have to start showing her your routine with the baby, and give her a little push once in a while. For me, it's vital to set your standards and expectations on that first day. Before her shift ends, give her a piece of paper with some notes and explain to her the things you've written down. Tell her that your house and system is unique, and you appreciate her understanding with this.

b. Observe, and don't leave her alone for the first week. Then gradually let her be alone with your baby until you feel comfortable with her ability to meet all of your child's needs.

c. Expect your baby to miss you and cling on to you during the process. A baby might cry, but it is okay. They will get used to it.

d. "Your baby will be closer to the yaya than you if you do this." This is the most incorrect statement I have ever read. Your baby is yours and knows you by instinct, smell, voice and your heartbeat, so, new Momshies, don't ever worry about this.

e. Your baby is smart enough to know their parents. My baby, Seiya, at 7 months, already recognized and realized that his parents were unique. As his parents, we always make sure to bond with him when we can during the day, even when the *yaya* is around.

Choose a pediatrician who can entertain your questions and messages online

a. You need a patient practitioner who will be there for you and understand your concerns. DO NOT become a hypochondriac and think your baby is unwell all the time. In some cases use your instincts, and ride out the situation until you know that you need your pediatrician's help.

b. There are some nights that paranoia will kick in, and you will have questions running around in your mind that only a professional can answer. Be calm when this happens, and write them down so you can discuss them calmly with your pediatrician. I was fortunate to be able to message Seiya's pediatrician even during the night to give me peace of mind. It's a huge help and relief to know that a pediatrician is always there for me and my little one.

Join a motherhood community online

a. There are tons of Facebook groups for mothers online, but only a few are worthy to be a part of. Just be wary and smart when joining a group. Don't get caught up in competition discussions, and make sure that you are engaging with people who are like-minded. It is very important to feel part of a collective, and there is always encouragement in these circumstances.

b. On the brighter side, a decent Facebook or online group can give you the support that you need to move forward as a mom. It's also easy access for research about baby topics, parenting styles and family travels. It is also a hub where you will find that you are literally not alone because you will soon realize that so many people are going through similar experiences as you. I felt a warm welcome when I joined one particular group; I felt their virtual hugs and open hearts. It feels so good to know that other Momshies understand how I feel and what I think. The comfort that a support group brings can ease up your burdens.

c. Talking to somebody can make you feel good, but as a mom, we rarely even have the time for ourselves, so talking online is actually very convenient and practical.

d. If you need help, please join my online group — the Gomomshie.com support group on Facebook. A lot of moms, or members of the group, will help you right away. It's amazing! We can't wait to see you there.

e. I'd recommend these kinds of online groups to those who love to share, so they can read some experiences of other mothers around the world, like the ones in the next page.

Testimonials

"I became a mom at the early age of 21. When something unfamiliar to you suddenly happens, it becomes scary and challenging, but my experience taught me to be humble and accept that I can't do it alone. Thank God my mother is with me. Her presence and support, especially during my son's infant to toddler years, has made me feel safe and secure every step of the way. My mom boosts my confidence; it's fun to explore and okay to make mistakes from this journey because she's got my back. We may not always see eye to eye in terms of parenting style, but remember when they say 'an apple doesn't fall far from the tree'? One way or another, I got it from my momma. It may just be version 2.0."

—Jessica Ador, mom of a teenager

"When Lucca isn't feeling well, he always looks for me and my mom. And I'm forever grateful that my mom is there with me throughout this motherhood journey. She gives comfort to me and Lucca. It's also such a relief to know that somebody is absolutely there to help me and back me up in taking care of my little one."

—Rox Romero, a first-time mom

Co-Parenting is Real

Let me remind you of something, Momshies. You did not bring your baby into this world alone; somebody helped you with it and that is your partner or husband, or even your ex. Co-parenting means that you take care of your little one regardless of your marital status. You are in this together, and knowing that the responsibility of your child belongs to both of you will pave the way to a successful formula for when you need each other during the good and bad times. And there will be some very testing times as well, so this is where your skills as a team come into play. You both want what's best for your baby, so in order to succeed, you have to commit to winning for the betterment of your baby.

Having a partner in life, who is an active partner in looking after the baby, can make you 50% less tired, and a system of duties that work between you and your partner can make parenting a lot more manageable. This way, there can never be an argument about who did more or less. Writing things down and implementing a schedule for both of you will create a transparent, bird's eye view of what you both need to do in order to succeed.

It's shocking to me to see some reactions online like, *"Oh, you're so lucky to have a husband who wakes up in the middle of the night to carry, sway, and feed the baby."* It is NOT luck, Momshies. It is a partner owning his responsibility as a father.

However, we also need to consider our partners' feelings when it comes to parenting. If it's their first time, know that it is also confusing for them as well as challenging and overwhelming for all involved. The first time embarking on anything new can be quite overwhelming. Don't be afraid to give your partner some roles, and responsibility. He also deserves to bond with his child and also to be able for him to experience fatherhood in the most loving way.

- ★ *changing diapers*
- ★ *swaying your baby to sleep*
- ★ *reading your little one some books*
- ★ *giving your baby a bath*
- ★ *burping the baby*
- ★ *feeding the baby with a bottle*

List down 5 things that you'd like your partner to help you with that will lessen the burden for you

1. _____

2. _____

3. _____

4. _____

5. _____

If your partner is away during the day for work, let them do some of these tasks when they get home or even during the night. Don't let him go to bed without touching the baby or bonding with the baby. It's important to include your partner in these situations because you're partners. Again, you made your little one together, so enjoy these moments with your baby because time goes by really fast. Before you know it, your baby will be walking, talking and running!

If you're both working parents, all the more reason for you to share some tasks or responsibilities after work so you're NOT both burnt out.

Testimonials

"My partner played a big part in why I didn't suffer from postpartum depression (PDD). He showed me so much genuine care. He was true to his word when he said that he'd own his responsibility as the father of our child; that he would always be there to help me out in better or worse situations. When I was awake in the middle of the night, he would also wake up with us and help me out in taking care of our little one. I'm so blessed to have him in my life".

—Irene Llagas, a first-time mom

I feel so grateful and blessed because I have a loving partner in life who also takes care of us. He also makes sure the kids are in shape when I'm tired from online meetings."

—Ina Somoza, a mom of two

'Me Time'
not "Mommy Time" or "Wife Time"
Think about yourselves, Momshies!!

Mothers tend to give so much of themselves, and when they give all of the time, they spread themselves too thin, leading to exhaustion. When we give, we must also receive!

You've been pregnant and given birth; your body and soul need a treat once in a while. A lot of mothers ignore the fact that self-care is paramount and an integral, as well as necessary, aspect of motherhood. You can give more love and care to your little one if you love and care for yourself first. Remember, you can only give what you have in your tank. You have to learn how to fill that regularly in order to be a better mother or wife. You want to be a race car with ample fuel, not a rusty old tanker that keeps breaking down because of pressure and exhaustion. Remember to look after yourself, so you can always be at the forefront of your baby's needs.

⚠ Suggestions and Practical Tips for Self-Care ⚠

MEDITATION
If you have the time in the morning, or even before you go to sleep, meditate for thirty minutes to one hour and you will feel peace and calmness within you. It might seem like a big chunk of time to spend on mediation, but let me tell you something, Momshies. Without calmness of mind you will be running on empty, and in the end you'll feel wiped out and your baby will certainly feel it too.

You may include yoga during meditation. There are lots of available relaxing yoga and meditations on YouTube or online. Search for the one that you align with, so you don't give up.

I can't tell you how much exercise helps me to stay strong and active throughout this motherhood journey. Exercise is one of my best friends, and I am committed to movement like I am to my baby and my marriage. Releasing endorphins will certainly make you a much happier Momshie. Exercise can come in many different forms; swimming, aerobics, CrossFit, Zumba dancing, playing tennis or badminton. All of these can help you improve your physical strength and help you clear your mind. Plus, it will help you get outside where you can meet some new people from your community.

KEEP YOUR BODY MOVING, MOMSHIE!

Before pregnancy, I was going to the gym almost every day to exercise and maintain the body shape I wanted for myself. When I got pregnant, I stopped gradually until I started my motherhood journey. For the first couple of months after giving birth, my doctor didn't allow me to exercise because I gave birth via cesarean section, and I had to be careful about infections and post-birth complications.

Once she gave me the clearance to do some stretching exercises, I took the opportunity to begin my fitness journey again. Walking was the best option for me to start again before I got back into weights and vigorous exercise. However, on some days my body was saying something different to me; *"I'm TOO tired to exercise!"*

Is this phrase familiar, Momshies? Well, you are not alone. I feel the same. Actually, I felt the same. After the birth, I felt weak and had no energy to even think about moving my body and start working out again. I told myself that carrying or lifting my baby and dancing or playing with him all day long was considered exercise. This is partially true, but it was just an excuse to tell myself to NOT take care of my body and self.

Then one day, I couldn't carry my little one for more than two minutes because I was getting a backache, and it seemed like I had no more strength in my body to even carry my baby. I was having a hard time coping with the weight of my child. That was when I realized that maybe I wasn't taking care of my own body properly.

I decided to get back to my fitness routine and hired a fitness instructor who could coach me for one hour, every other day. I needed someone who could focus on me — not only for the purpose of my body-shape and vanity, but, most importantly, to help me to improve my body's strength. Try and slice out an hour of your day, or even half an hour to begin exercise. It's hard, but it's worth it. Physical strength definitely helps with mental power, and it gave me more energy to do more tasks during the day. Think of exercise as an investment in yourself and for your family. A strong Momshie is indeed a happy Momshie.

It's all in the mind, Momshies!
Remember, being strong is the new sexy!

PAMPER YOURSELF WITH A MASSAGE!
After all the changes our body has endured, it deserves an aromatic massage once in a while. Massages encourage blood circulation and flow, and the movement of the chi energy in your body makes you happy. I don't know about you, but massages really helped me recover faster from my surgery after giving birth. I also feel a lot happier after a massage — I feel like I am in bliss, and this state is definitely transposed to my son, who can feel pure joy emitting from me when I have taken some time to care for myself.

DRESS UP AND PUT SOME MAKEUP ON!
I have to be completely honest with you, Momshies. I lost my passion for dressing up and wearing makeup post birth and while nursing my little one. I just thought that I didn't have the time or even a reason to dress up.

Every time I saw myself in the mirror, I always wondered, "Why do I always look like a mess?" Sometimes, I didn't even recognize myself anymore. On some days it looked like I didn't take a bath for a week, even though I had. So, one morning, I just decided to get out of my pajamas, and I started dressing up, fixing my hair and wearing some light makeup, even though I was staying at home. Wow! I can't tell you how a little bit of effort and making myself look good made me feel. I was suddenly so happy and felt like I was in my element. I began to feel much happier and more productive. That's the effect of self-care. I felt less tired and started to feel energized and more aligned.

DO WHAT YOU LOVE!
Beyond motherhood, we all have something we love to do; we have all had a passionate desire about a certain hobby we love, or just an activity we engage in because it fills up our soul with happiness. The activity you pursue with passion is going to make you less tired because you love it, and it makes you happy. It's also a part of self-care.

If you like to draw, do it! If you love to travel, do it! If you love to film some videos, do it! If you love trying different foods, do it! Don't think about it, just do it!

Being a mother entails sacrifice. Sometimes we tend to neglect what we love because we feel as though all our time needs to be spent caring for our baby, but my suggestion is for you to make a habit of setting a time for yourself to do what you love. Again, understanding and actually doing what you love can help you understand yourself better as a person while looking after your needs as well.

Testimonials

"My husband is my support; my child is my drive and inspiration; my parents are my guidance; my job is my passion. But self-care is

what keeps me sane. So, for me, self-care is a priority, and it can be as simple as drinking a glass of water or as grand as having a full body massage at a resort spa."

—Mikee Suarez-Labrador, a first-time mom

"As a new mom, I really thought that 'me time' was not really important. However, as time passes by, I've noticed that I'm feeling tired all the time, feeling ugly and feeling unworthy sometimes. So, I've revisited the things I did before I became a mom, like going to a salon and doing some shopping. 'Me time' is really important; it may be a minute or an hour, but it helps a lot. Also, the effect of a massage after giving birth is surreal. I can't explain how much joy it brought to my life."

—Erika Santos-Camson, a first time mom

WORKSHEET

List reasons why you feel tired

_____

_____

_____

_____

_____

_____

_____

_____

_____

_____

List down all the things you will do to increase
and rev up your energy

_____

_____

_____

_____

_____

_____

_____

_____

_____

_____

_____

_____

_____

_____

_____

_____

_____

_____

_____

_____

_____

_____

_____

_____

Ask for help
Who are you going to ask for help?

_____

_____

_____

_____

_____

Husband & Wife/Partner Teamwork
Create a list that highlights duties and
responsibilities. Make it fun! For example, clean the
baby's cot while listening to music, and dance like
nobody's watching.

_____

_____

_____

_____

_____

_____

_____

_____

_____

_____

_____

_____

ME Time
What activities will I engage in to promote self-care?

_____

_____

_____

_____

_____

_____

_____

_____

_____

_____

_____

_____

_____

_____

GO
MOMSHIE
LITTLE SECRET

Here is a little hidden secret that I want to offer you. I use this affirmation all the time when I'm feeling down and, I promise you, it works wonders. Read it, and then type it up or write it down. Stick it on your mirror or fridge, or maybe even near your baby's cot. You could put it next to your bedside. Repeat it every day until you feel it.

I AM A MOM

I GAVE BIRTH TO A WONDERFUL CHILD.

It's normal that I feel tired sometimes, but it's never okay that I feel TOO tired.

I WILL NOW MAKE A PACT WITH MYSELF TO MAKE SURE THAT I'LL FIND THE TIME TO DO THE THINGS THAT MAKE ME A BETTER MOMSHIE.

Then I can be happier, healthier and take care of my family with a grateful heart, a serene soul and an energized body.

I am important.

I have dreams and aspirations.

I am grateful to be a parent.

I am blessed to be responsible

for another life.

I am in love with my baby.

I am in love with my partner.

I am in love with myself.

CHAPTER 2

Figuring it Out as We Go along

When I was pregnant, I realized that I knew nothing about raising a child. I was totally overwhelmed by the prospect of raising my own flesh and blood. I am one of the many who decided to talk to other mothers and scour the internet for information.

Upon reading some stories and experiences online, the pressure did get to me. I felt like what I read made my head spin, and there was no room for error. I felt like I was expected to be a supermom. I knew this couldn't be the right path, and in order to alleviate my anxiety, I joined a few seminars to educate myself on the trials and triumphs of motherhood. I was obsessed with wanting to know everything before the arrival of the baby, and it was obvious that I was spiraling when my friends and family saw the pressure get to me. But I kept telling myself that it was pretty normal to feel this way, especially for first time moms.

When my baby was born, from dawn until evening or even for the whole 24 hours, my duties seemed never-ending. From breastfeeding, bathing my little one, playing with him, cooking for the family, cleaning the house, putting the baby down for a nap, doing laundry, hanging the clothes to dry, washing dishes, taking care of my husband, taking a shower, getting my little one to sleep and, again, breastfeeding him once in a while through the night… *Pheeewwww!* It was always such a long day and night. All I was really missing was my red cape so I could officially title myself as 'supermom'.

I was doing this routine on my own for quite some time, and it was exhausting as well as frustrating. But then one night, I asked myself, "Is this how I'm supposed to feel? Should I keep on doing this to be a supermom?" Some mothers and some stories online were telling me that it was all normal; that was how a mother should be, *must be* and I would get used to it. However, why did I feel so unhappy and tired? I was completely zapped of my energy.

One morning, I woke up realizing that I was living a life that other moms had set out for me. I was under the influence of *their* stories and what society wanted me to do. On that day, when I woke up from feeling like a slave, I reassessed my situation and adjusted to the parenting style I wanted. I started to take note of what actually worked for my baby and me, and with a little bit of intuition, I turned my situation around to suit my unique situation and child.

If you're a mom and you feel immense pressure, always know that you should not live up to the expectations of other people. You don't have to do what other people have done or are doing. Your motherhood journey, like mine, is unique, and you can do it in your own way.

If you want to take that pressure off yourself, here are some suggestions that can be of use.

Keep. Things. Simple.

Motherhood is complicated enough, so don't overcomplicate things. The pressure and influence from so many people around you can make your life as a new mom harder to manage, too hectic and more stressful.

Look at yourself and honestly ask, "Do I overcomplicate things? Especially by trying to emulate what other mothers do?" Are you receiving too much information and giving yourself burn-out while trying to delve into the next big study? This is not a race, Momshies. You need to learn to work at your own pace. Keeping things simple in motherhood is important. It will also give you time to focus more on the important things in life. Don't over-think everything, as this is unhealthy.

Learn to Say NO

Being a mother is a lot of things. You can be the friendliest mom in the whole world by talking to a lot of moms out there; you can be a mom who loves to entertain people; and you can be a mom who loves to listen and gain knowledge from others' expertise. Remember that whatever kind of mom you are, you should learn to choose your friends and community wisely.

When it is time to say no, make sure you exercise your power to create boundaries. "No" is such a small little word, but it carries great weight with the notion of sticking up for yourself when you don't want to be in a certain situation.

Surround yourself with people who uplift you, not the people who pull you down and who end up becoming a toxic influence in your life. Learn how to say, "No!" when it is necessary. There are moments that other moms, or even some of your friends, can make you feel sad or less worthy. Don't let that happen to you; don't be afraid to cut ties and start new relationships. Learn to say, "Stop," and, "Enough is enough."

Start Praising and Stop Criticizing

Motherhood becomes very complicated when one starts to criticize another. Keep things simple by giving your fellow

Momshies encouragement. It's really that simple — be kind. If you can't find the respite you need within an encouraging environment, then go out and keep searching for a community who shares the same mindset as you.

Managing your Expectations:
Keep it Real, Keep it Simple

You're a mom. You can do things but *not* everything, and you have to know that having limits is okay. As long as you keep your expectations real, it's unlikely you'll be disappointed in other people or yourself. It's important that you don't let yourself be disappointed, as this will lead to unhappiness and doubt. Create a set of daily goals; things that are manageable within your circumstances and schedule. Never expect too much from other people because if you do, you let the pressure from other people enter your lives, and that will not make your life simple.

Practice Minimalism

I'm beyond guilty when I say that first time moms tend to buy a lot of things for their baby, especially when we're influenced by other people like the celebrities who we're following online. Being a minimalist does not mean being stingy for your baby but instead learning to buy enough so that the needs of your little ones are met. Keep things simple and less fancy. This way you can focus on important facets of bringing up a child, which include great healthcare and education. You don't need the latest pram, bib, booties or jewelry for your baby. It's unnecessary, and they grow out of these materialistic things very quickly.

Simplicity is not a one-size-fits-all phenomenon. All these suggestions can work for you, but some may not. You have to define what simplicity means to you and how much you are willing to save and spend for your baby's future.

Living the Quiet Life

Who does not want to have a peaceful life? I can safely say that we all want a life of serenity. Who doesn't? When I became a mom, I received so many messages online from people who I rarely knew. Some of them were giving me so many tips or suggestions on how to handle my own child, and some of them were simply just asking about my experiences. I also joined different mom communities online and offline to keep myself updated on things about parenting and motherhood. So from one small circle, my life has expanded into a big one. It doesn't have to be a negative experience, but there are consequences when you open yourself up to a wider community because your life will become a focus for so many more people.

You may think that having a quiet life is impossible when you have a baby. Indeed, raising a child and living with a baby will make your home loud and crazy sometimes. Peace can only be achieved when the little one is asleep. Sometimes, and I'm guilty of this, I just want to hide and stay in a locked bedroom by myself, so I can feel peaceful, away from children's songs, loud cries and worries. The last thing I want to add to my life is unnecessary noise or unsolicited influence from other people.

So yes, finding peace might seem an impossible dream, but it's possible if we can manage our life at the level at which we want it to be. You choose who becomes a part of your tribe, Momshies, and you make the ultimate decision about who you want to spend your time with. Time is a commodity, just like the air we breathe, so make sure you are spending time with people who uplift you, encourage you and who show you their genuine side.

GO MOMSHIE
LITTLE SECRET

Living a quiet life means fewer distractions, less people, less clutter and less influence.

It can be quite amazing to live a quiet life in this world of rushing around and noises. You don't have to run away and be on top of a mountain. All you need to do is maneuver your way around your life; where you acknowledge the times you need to be away from all of the noise so you and your baby can ultimately bond.

Manage your Calendar

Instead of adding more things to your to-do list, make it a habit to reserve some available slots during the week for yourself to do things that you love to do. Marking your calendars to make a living or making your life super busy with errands may crush your soul, and you will end up not having a life. Less things on your calendar means a quieter life for you. Try it by crossing off the things that you don't want to do. It's a liberating feeling, and you will begin to feel empowered because the choice to do most things in life is in your hands.

Practice Intimate Social Conversation

What I mean is one-on-one communication with a friend or loved one. If you have the urge to socialize, make it intimate or limited to one couple. In this way, you protect yourself from overcrowding and from having to entertain or talk to a lot of people where you may waste unnecessary energy. Having an intimate social conversation can develop deeper understanding and bonding, and it fosters quality time.

Go for Quality Rather than Quantity

A few real friends are worth having over thousands of fake ones. As a mom, you will soon realize who will stick with you and help you through the day. We seek a lot of comfort and help from the people closest to us, especially if you're a first-time mom. It's okay to have a small circle of friends who will be there to back you up and listen to your problems rather than you spending time on those who are always preoccupied with something else. You want to be around a circle of friends who don't put on a facade of 'supermom'; there is no such thing, Momshies. It will also give you a quiet life as there will be less drama, insecurity, problems and bragging rights. When you come across this scenario, where you feel pressured to conform, this would be the perfect time to swiftly and gracefully exit that community, and seek another one that is more in alignment with your own goals as a new parent.

Embrace Change

The best way to take off the pressure and become free from the influence of other people is to embrace change. When you learn to evolve and shift as well as to adapt, you will soon learn that motherhood becomes a fun learning experience, not a mundane feeling of a jack-in-the-box who wants to hide most of time, only resurfacing when 'wound up' by someone else.

Gandhi said, "Be the change you wish to see in the world." With this mantra we become evolving women, who ultimately become revolutionaries because we know the true meaning of learning to adapt and go with the flow.

Embracing shifts, twists and turns will render you a resilient Momshie with more confidence, which in turn makes you more innovative. When my little one was born, my mother helped me by taking care of my baby for a couple of months while I recovered from the surgery. There were moments that my mom resisted change. She kept on telling me how she used to do things for us when we were her babies. It was hard for her to see me do something else other than following her ways. Her resistance affected me in a way that meant I doubted myself every time I wanted to try something new.

Eventually, I made a decision to gently stand up to her and, at times, do the opposite of what she was suggesting. Some of her ways were so old fashioned, I just couldn't handle her archaic style. I had to find a lot of courage to get out of my mom's old paradigm and create some changes for myself and my little one. When this happens to you, make sure that you tell the other person that there's no hard feelings towards them and you appreciate their help, but this time around you are going to do your best and follow your own intuition.

GO MOMSHIE
LITTLE SECRET

Sphere of Control

This is the concept of things we're worried about. Things that we have control over; things we can influence; and things that are outside of our control. Remember that you have the power to navigate your life, and your sphere of control is monitored and maneuvered by you! So, take control over your life, and know that ultimately you are not alone. The sphere is reminiscent of your little world and who and what you have in it. Choose wisely and confidently.

I would like to share a funny story with you, my dear readers. Unconsciously, I had been taking over and controlling the whole house, especially the things that related to, or affected, my little one. My husband once said that whenever I demanded something to be changed, he would look at my mom, and they would nod at each other behind my back. It has now become their hidden language to highlight whenever I'm being bossy over my little one's schedules and general things. They're not against me; they both agreed that all the changes I wanted to enforce were all reasonable and needed, but they were just surprised at how I was slowly morphing into a "boss lady" and taking control of the house. It's something that all moms are capable of. Taking the lead to protect and offer the best care possible for our child.

Take. Your. Time. The pressure is off when you take your time and grow at your own pace. Motherhood is an endless journey; you can't memorize it overnight. You will figure it out as you go, so take your time. Flowers don't grow in a day and neither will your babies, or you. Be patient and kind to yourself, and learn to move and tango your way through motherhood with a smile on your face. Time is on your side, only if you want it to be. Don't forget to go back into your diary today, and cross off some things that are **not necessary** at this time for your growth as a new mom.

When I was pregnant, I was worried that I wouldn't grasp everything I needed to do before I gave birth. Now that I have given birth and am currently taking care of my baby, I'm stressed out that I might have missed something important in order to nourish and nurture my baby properly. The pressure within me, and from people around me, was growing because I was feeling the need to rush into knowing everything at once. Hurrying all the time creates stress and unhappiness, so it's better to take our time and learn as we go.

But how can we possibly take our time when our baby grows up so fast? Simple, just take your time. Motherhood is not a race.

Time Management

If you can manage your time properly, things will fall into place, which will allow you to accomplish and learn more than you expect.

Make it a habit to plan your day ahead in order to prepare properly and prevent some wasted time and opportunities. When you also manage your time efficiently, it will help you to focus on important matters rather than reading unnecessary information on the internet (or engage in brainless browsing on your Instagram or Facebook feed or stories).

I always have a notebook planner with me. What I do is update it every night when the baby is asleep and plan for the next day. It always gives me a clear, bird's eye view of what to expect and what I could do. It helps me to be more productive and to know when I can have some free time for myself. Jotting down the things you want to learn and want to do for your baby helps keep order, while pacing yourself to avoid exhaustion.

Stop beating yourself up, Momshie. We are all a work in progress, but we learn eventually that we will get there by understanding more concepts for the betterment of your little one.

Worksheets for Finding Out Where You Need To Improve

Know your triggers. Write down all the sources of current pressure in your life. Be completely honest. It can be a person or situation

_____

_____

_____

_____

_____

_____

_____

Now write down all the people who greatly influence you with your parenting style. Write down why they are important in your learning curve as a new Momshie

1. _____

2. _____

3. _____

What are the specific things that you can do in order to ease off some pressure and influence in your life, to start learning things at your own pace and time?

_____

_____

_____

_____

_____

_____

_____

_____

_____

_____

_____

_____

Define your idea of 'simplicity'. What will make your life more minimal in order to stop some chaos around you?

_____

_____

_____

_____

_____

_____

_____

_____

_____

_____

_____

Write down five ideas you can implement NOW to embrace change.

1. _____

2. _____

3. _____

4. _____

5. _____

Repeat this statement until you feel it, and sign it as a contract with yourself. Print this page out and stick it somewhere where you can see it. Show it to a loved one, so they can hold you accountable.

**I am a mom and I feel pressured
when people and society are telling me
what I should and should not do.**

**Upon reading this chapter, I promise that I will be
the kind of mother that I want for myself, and I
will practice a method of unique motherhood that
works for me and my baby and for my family.**

**I will free myself from the influence of other
people and even from the influence of people
closest to me. I will ease up on myself by taking my
time and learning about motherhood as we go. I
will embrace change and keep things simple to live
a quiet and peaceful life.**

NAME IN FULL:

_____

SIGNATURE:

_____

DATE:

_____

IN WITNESS OF:

_____

CHAPTER 3

We are all Trying to get Stronger

Our body goes through a lot of major changes during pregnancy and childbirth. I'm always amazed at the kind of expansion our body goes through to accommodate a new life. Make sure that you give your body full credit for being a masterpiece of true metamorphosis, Momshie! And don't forget that before, during and after pregnancy, your remarkable body deserves a whole lot of love and care.

It is so true when people say that a woman's body will never be the same after giving birth. Hell yes! It is even stronger and better. I've developed so much respect for my body despite the stretch marks and some imperfections.

But let's all face reality here — postpartum recovery is hard. It's hard for our bodies and for us in general. In this book, I'm going to talk about postpartum problems, but in this chapter, let me talk about our temple — our body.

Some doctors say that you need six to eight weeks for your body to recover from giving birth. Don't listen to that advice because it actually takes nine months to a year for your body to go through the whole process of shifting everything back to its normal place. It took us nine months to grow our babies, so it makes sense to think it will take about the same amount of time for our body to re-group to its original composition. But some of us take even longer, and that's completely okay.

Mother Nature bestows upon us to prioritize our baby over our own needs, and it starts when we hold our baby in our hands for the first time. All the pain goes away and you just start taking care of the baby even though your episiotomy stitches are still fresh and there is still blood flowing through the catheter.

I gave birth via C-Section, and they say that the body's recovery in this situation takes even longer than someone who has given birth normally. Looking back, it's amazing how I managed to get up so many times in the middle of the night to breastfeed my baby knowing that there was a real possibility of my abdominal stitches rupturing if I strained myself. I have a strong, stubborn personality when it comes to dealing with pain — I always do things normally until I feel pain. If I don't feel anything, I will keep on doing things as if everything is fine.

I'm not saying all, but I think many mothers are like me. We numb ourselves in order to do things for our baby, and that's not entirely okay. I agree that we have to do what keeps our baby alive and happy, but what concerns me is when we start ignoring ourselves, especially when we are in the process of recovery.

As I mentioned, I was ignoring my stitches and getting in and out of bed and carrying my baby all the time as if I hadn't had a C-section. Then I had my six weeks postpartum check up with my OBGYN. She removed my binder to check my abdomen, and she started pressing and checking to see if there was pain. There was. Until that moment, I hadn't realized that I'd been forcing my body and neglecting myself because I was pushing myself to over-achieve and, since I didn't feel any pain, I made myself go on. This is a dangerous and slippery slope to be on. Please don't ever push yourself to a limit where you can ultimately jeopardize you or your baby's health. Since then, I've tried to be more mindful of my body. I realized the hard way that I had to recover fully first in order to give my best self to my baby.

If you are trying to recover from giving birth, I want you to know that it takes time, but you will get there. It may be hard at first, and it may seem impossible for your body to feel strong again like you did before pregnancy. However, I want you to know this right now. It's possible. But, it's entirely up to you.

Here are things that you can do in order to recover fully.

Say goodbye to the "Endure Mindset"

The trials that come with motherhood manifest in different forms, and one of them is the pain of recovery after giving birth. Our body is in pain, but some women try to endure it because they believe that it's all part of motherhood. No, it is not! Some pain *can* be endured, but postpartum pain must be cured and healed, so please don't ignore it or try to endure it. I suggest removing that 'endure and get used to it' mindset of yours when dealing with postpartum recovery and replacing it with a 'proactive mindset'.

We've all heard that saying, "It's all in the mind," and our mind does work powerfully during postpartum recovery. When we feel pain, our mind says, "Do something about it." Once your mindset changes with regards to dealing with your body, the more you can take care of your body properly and thus garner a faster recovery.

Stop acting like a martyr by enduring all the pain. There's no prize for a mother who can endure so much discomfort that it hinders her ability to take care of her baby. Stop acting as if you did not have surgery or stitches on your vagina. It bloody hurts! Nobody is counting the times you spend playing or holding your baby. Focus on your recovery, Momshie. Rest well and find the proper time to take care of your body in order to heal faster.

Remember, prioritizing yourself is never selfish. It is necessary to fill your energy tank so you're prepared and ready to give more for your little one. Looking after yourself on three levels — body, mind and soul — will make motherhood so much easier. Plus, we hear all the time that there are scientific reasons behind the rest and recovery that athletes undertake when they are injured, to repair and strengthen their bodies. The same must apply to us during this fragile time in our lives.

Honestly, you may endure postpartum pain for a little while, but your body might still break down. Maybe not right away, but it will catch up with you in the future. So, set your mindset right when dealing with postpartum pain and recovery. As a former flight attendant, I am reminded that during an emergency routine, passengers must put on their own oxygen mask first before putting on their kid's oxygen mask. Similarly, you must take care of yourself, Momshies, in order to then take care of your little ones more efficiently.

Create a support system

Engaging with numerous people in your life, whom you consider important, can greatly influence you in a positive way. Creating a support system is important in order to recover physically and mentally after giving birth. It will be your source of energy, wisdom and comfort during your postpartum recovery.

GO
MOMSHIE
LITTLE SECRET

We are not created to face motherhood alone.

There are people around us who can stay with us and help us get through the day during this motherhood journey. I wouldn't be fully recovered by now without the support system I built during my postpartum journey, and for this I am forever grateful.

A support system includes a few people you trust who are willing to help you recover faster by lifting some burdens off your shoulders. They are the ones you're comfortable talking to and who make your day brighter than the day before. It can be your partner or husband, your trusted friends, family members, doctors, pastors, financial advisors or fellow moms.

I gave birth during the COVID-19 pandemic in 2020. Almost all countries around the world practiced community quarantine and social distancing. This meant that all my relatives and friends couldn't visit me or the baby; face-to-face contact was prohibited as a way of preventing the risk of viral transmission. Given the circumstances, I relied upon a support system which included only two people — my mom and my husband. Fortunately, they were both strong enough to support me, to lift me up when I was feeling down, to help me rest, clean my wounds, take care of the baby, manage the house and to calm my nerves when I was feeling stressed out. They continue to do this for me on a daily basis.

They are the reason I have a better coping mechanism and less worry. They pushed me to walk so I could recover faster from the C-section, and they reminded me to slow down when I was moving too fast. They helped care for my cesarean scars and ease my aches and pains. They really served as my overall source of joy and encouragement, and for that I'll be forever thankful, with all my heart.

If you want to start building your support system, you can start reaching out to people, before you give birth, who make you happy and whom you can trust. You just have to be willing to accept help and take an interest in other peoples' initiatives and efforts.

Some neighbors can even show support by sharing some food with you for lunch and dinner. I can't tell you enough how much this could help you when there's a newborn in the house. A simple gesture like this, even from a distant friend or relative, is so appreciated.

Start a healthy habit

When you're still feeling some bodily discomforts, it's really hard to initiate change or start a new habit. However, it is important to start new healthy habits right after giving birth, as it will make you even stronger and help you to recover faster.

Some women stop taking prenatal vitamins right after giving birth. Why? The reason may be beyond my comprehension, but the thought of not taking care of yourself because there's no baby inside you anymore is wrong.

Do you remember the day you discovered that you were pregnant? And do you remember what the doctor told you about dos and don'ts?

I clearly remember the changes I had to make when I learned that I was pregnant. I immediately stopped fasting and ate a healthy balanced diet three times a day and some snacks in between. I made sure that there were some healthy veggies in my meals and that I also had enough carbohydrates in my diet. I also became conscious about what I drank, abstaining from alcohol and even coffee. Of course, I had to give in to some of my unhealthy cravings, but I made sure that it didn't become a habit because I wanted to share a greater amount of healthy nutrition with the baby in my womb. I realized that during pregnancy I started living a healthy life and, even after Seiya's birth, I realized I couldn't find a reason why I should stop doing it, especially when I was dealing with postpartum recovery.

What is a healthy habit? It's a practice that you initiate in order for your mind and body to function at its best. It also means taking control of circumstances around you that could affect your life. Here are some simple suggestions:

Food: Whatever you allow to enter your body affects you greatly. Eating food is a big part of our day and we need it for staying alive. If you eat trash, you feel like trash, so if you want to start feeling better, you should start taking in the proper amount of healthy foods that could help your muscles, bones and body become stronger. I'd suggest starting to eat organic foods rich in protein, like chicken breast, eggs, spinach and avocado. You may consult with a nutritionist or do your own research online, so you can control what you put into your body. Having a healthy balanced diet can also give you the authority to control your weight; it can help you lose that pregnancy belly if you make it a habit to eat a healthy balanced diet.

Eat well, but don't start your slimming diet yet. It's important that your body takes in the food needed in order to ease the pain, fatigue and constipation. Your body needs to be healthy first before it gets into the shape you want it to be. Be kind to your body, as I mentioned; it's a temple you should respect.

Exercise: This is a tough one, especially when you feel vulnerable after giving birth. Abdominal stitches and episiotomy stitches are no joke — they can make us want to lie in bed for days on end. However, you should start doing some light stretches and movements as soon as one day after giving birth. I was advised to walk slowly around the hospital room whenever I could in order to exercise my muscles and for my body to realize that it can still function after the shocking pain and medications it received during childbirth.

"You have to keep moving," is the phrase I always keep in mind, and it's what I did right after giving birth, but with precaution. You know yourself more than anybody else — you know your limits — so you must stop if you think you've moved enough. Your physical recovery really depends on you.

Supplements: I have mentioned the topic of prenatal vitamins earlier. Don't stop taking them right after giving birth. It is important to continue to do so during recovery and to maintain this practice as a healthy habit. If you're nursing your little one, it's even more important for you to continue taking them, as you need to enrich your nutrient intake for your breast milk.

Another common problem for mothers is when they become anemic due to heavy bleeding during childbirth. Taking iron supplements or eating food rich in iron can help you prevent anemia, and this can also make your energy and mood levels higher and better. Taking calcium supplements also can definitely help you to recover faster, as your body needs it to build and maintain strong bones. There are many other supplements that you can take; however, make sure to always consult your doctor to see if it's safe for breastfeeding moms or if it's safe for your specific medical conditions.

Starting a healthy habit can give you so many benefits. Most especially, providing you with the energy and the physical ability you need to care for your little one.

Sleep when you can

I know it's almost impossible to get some sleep when you have just had a baby, but it's important to have some whenever you can, as it will allow you to recover faster.

This is when your support system comes in. You must give permission to let somebody else help you in taking care of your baby in order for you to get a good night's sleep. This will help to rejuvenate your body. You may need someone to help you in the middle of the day or during the night. You may even just need someone to give you some respite for 30 minutes or one hour. Grab that opportunity and sleep; it helps you to build energy so you can take care of your baby better and make wiser decisions throughout the day. Lack of sleep will render you moody, and it will be a disservice to your baby.

When you hear people say, *"You should also sleep when your baby is asleep"*, take heed of this advice because it is a real thing, and I did this until I recovered. I didn't care if there was a pile of laundry to be washed or a pile of dishes in the sink. I ignored all of those chores so that I could sleep. Please don't think it is being selfish or lazy — it's all part of your recovery. Again, Momshie, you need to sleep!

When I became a mom, I stopped staying up late to watch movies just because it was a Friday night. I had to shift my sleeping patterns because I knew that my little one would be waking up in the middle of the night to eat. I made sure to sleep early, or when the baby slept, so I would have enough rest and then be able to get up and feed my little one.

It's true that there are things that you have to sacrifice in order to sleep. Certain circumstances — house chores, hanging out with friends or family, or having to work — need to be put to one side. Sometimes, we have to choose if we should sleep or run some errands. You must prioritize sleep over anything else until you recover. Once your energy is back, you can go back to your usual speed and be ready for multitasking if some situations call for it.

Take it easy, be patient and get some sleep!

Worksheets for Your Development

What significant changes have you noticed in
your body after giving birth?

_____

_____

_____

_____

_____

_____

_____

_____

_____

_____

_____

_____

_____

_____

_____

_____

What are you planning to do in order to help your body to recover fully?

_____

_____

_____

_____

_____

_____

_____

_____

_____

_____

_____

_____

_____

_____

_____

_____

What healthy habits are you currently doing in order to recover faster?

_____

_____

_____

_____

_____

_____

_____

_____

_____

_____

_____

_____

_____

_____

_____

_____

_____

Print this page out and say these affirmations to yourself five times a day.

Write them down in a notebook. I have added seven sections here for you to practice writing these affirmations down for one week.

Please do this every day, and don't stop after seven days. After six weeks, if you make this a daily practice, you will indeed begin to see a shift in your mindset. It works. Trust me.

1. I respect my body.

2. My body is my temple.

3. I love and care for my body.

4. I am healthy.

5. I am supported.

6. I am patient and listen to my body's needs.

7. I have a proactive mindset.

8. I am positive and listen to the sounds around me.

9. I trust my intuition.

10. I know I have help around me.

MONDAY
DAY 1

1. _____

2. _____

3. _____

4. _____

5. _____

6. _____

7. _____

8. _____

9. _____

10. _____

 # TUESDAY
DAY 2

1. _____

2. _____

3. _____

4. _____

5. _____

6. _____

7. _____

8. _____

9. _____

10. _____

WEDNESDAY
DAY 3

1. _____
2. _____
3. _____
4. _____
5. _____
6. _____
7. _____
8. _____
9. _____
10. _____

THURSDAY
DAY 4

1. _____
2. _____
3. _____
4. _____
5. _____
6. _____
7. _____
8. _____
9. _____
10. _____

FRIDAY

DAY 5

1. _____

2. _____

3. _____

4. _____

5. _____

6. _____

7. _____

8. _____

9. _____

10. _____

 # SATURDAY
DAY 6

1. _____

2. _____

3. _____

4. _____

5. _____

6. _____

7. _____

8. _____

9. _____

10. _____

 # SUNDAY
DAY 7

1. _____
2. _____
3. _____
4. _____
5. _____
6. _____
7. _____
8. _____
9. _____
10. _____

GO
MOMSHIE
LITTLE SECRET

Dear Momshies,

   I'm writing this to give you a self-care prescription.

   Kindly take this once a day for the rest of your life.

   Say this with conviction:

I LOVE MYSELF & PROMISE TO LOOK AFTER MYSELF!

Yours sincerely,

Victoria

In the next few pages, I have outlined some tips for self-care that have helped me during my journey.

Self-care Prescription

Skin Care Routine

It's no secret that our skin is really important — it is what makes up most of our body, and it is the largest barrier against infection. Going through pregnancy and childbirth, our skin also experiences a different kind of stretching and pulling. During our postpartum recovery, we usually forget to include the skin on our face, legs, arms and belly, and who can blame us right? Moms, especially new moms, have very little time to themselves. Between caring for our baby, eating our meals and even sneaking in a few hours of sleep, there's not really any free time to do anything else, so it is inevitable that we forget about a regimented skin care routine.

I know it seems impossible, but I'm letting you know right now that there's a quick and simple way to take care of your skin. However, the only way it will perfectly work for you is if you've decided to include it in your morning and night routines and then stick with it.

I am not an expert dermatologist. I'm just simply giving you some of my personal tips that might work for you (but if you have very sensitive skin or are in any doubt, always consult an expert first).

When I was pregnant, I found some safe products I could use for pregnancy. Some of them enlightened me about the ingredients that could really make my skin look and feel healthier. So after I gave birth, I still continued to use them.

With the steps that I'm going to share with you, regardless of what specific products you use, they will ultimately help you to look your best, even when you're as busy as a bee.

STEP ONE: CLEANSE

You have to clean your skin first. Never skip cleaning your body with soap or water-based products for your face. I suggest looking for products with natural ingredients and a water solution. Avoid chemicals as much as possible.

For your body, look for a product that is already a combination of body wash and scrub. That way you will save time, but you'll still have clean and smooth skin.

For your face, look for a cleanser that has an exfoliating and brightening effect. Make sure to use a face cleanser appropriate for your skin type (dry, oily or sensitive). I had to switch to acne-friendly cleanser after giving birth to cure me of all my pregnancy acne; I'd never been so sensitive with products I'd used until I became a mom.

I always make sure that the products I apply to my skin are breastfeeding friendly, as I'm still currently nursing my little one.

STEP TWO: SERUM

For all the changes happening around us, there's always a tendency to be a stress ball, which then has a negative effect on our skin. It's not surprising to see ourselves in the mirror looking ten years older, especially when we neglect to apply serum to our face and have little or no sleep.

In order to rejuvenate your skin and look younger, consider looking for a serum that will hydrate your face, giving your skin a soft appearance. Facial serum products contain vitamins that can beat acne, dark spots and wrinkles. Anti-aging serum is available everywhere, and if you need one, go for it. You need that extra elasticity and collagen to keep your face young and fresh looking.

STEP THREE: MOISTURIZER

Apply a moisturizer to give you a refreshing feeling. This does not only apply to those who have dry skin. Moisturizer works really well at night. This can serve as your night cream to keep your skin tight and moisturized when you're having an all-nighter with your little one. This is the last step, as moisturizer holds water in the outermost layer of skin, and it also acts as a temporary barrier for the skin. This also improves your skin tone and texture, so if you want to keep your skin flawless and smooth, you may want to research some moisturizer products that might suit your skin type. For your body, I highly recommend some lotion or moisturizers that have oat or shea butter ingredients in them, as these feel really smooth on the skin.

Voila! That is your easy Go Momshie three-step skin care routine.

Important note: When choosing skin care products for yourself, keep in mind that mild, gentle, fragrance-free and natural products are your best choice because, like it or not, our skin has become extra sensitive after giving birth..

I must admit that I had great skin before I got pregnant — no pimples, no blackheads; just a few open pores here and there. I had no qualms about going out of the house with my bare face. When pregnancy happened, this was when my skin started to produce pimples (not only on my face, but also all over my back and chest). I was shocked and, not surprisingly, my confidence was affected. I didn't feel comfortable meeting other people or even showing my face to the crowd. I had tried different kinds of products that were obviously safe for pregnant or nursing women, but a lot of them didn't work. It was real torture on my skin until I found the right products for me.

During my postpartum recovery, I made sure to find the time to wash my face and apply serum and then moisturizer. Not only did it make my skin healthy, but it also made me feel happy, confident and pretty. Yes, it took a while before I was able to say, "I'm pretty," but I finally did.

My skin care routine may look simple, but that is what works for me — I have a super tight schedule every day. I love how quick and easy it is. It's completely done in two minutes. My advice is this: even if you have great skin post birth, it's still not a good excuse to not care for your skin. Having great skin just means that you must be able to maintain it. The only way you can do that is to establish, and then stick to, a routine that can nurture and nourish your beautiful skin.

Self-care Prescription

Healthy Meals

We all know that food is a necessity in life, and it's important to eat healthy food in order to live a balanced and nutritious life.

Self-care also applies to the food that you let yourself eat. Due to our busy schedule as a mom, it's often hard to find time to buy and prepare healthy food. Sometimes, we just give in to the rush and go for fast food, drive-thrus and food delivery. Quick and easy; that's what we want as a mom, isn't it? You may get it done, Momshie, but sooner or later, your junk food will certainly take its toll.

We have to understand that in order to meet the challenges of motherhood, whilst caring for our little one and ourselves, we have to start taking in nutritious meals and snacks. We all know this at the back of our minds, but it's really tough to actually do it and stick to it. I know, and I feel you.

Here are some healthy meal plans.

Let me go ahead and tell you not to worry. It isn't going to be all green and organic. Calm yourself down and read on.

MONDAY

BREAKFAST

Oatmeal with banana
Coffee/latte with soy
Almond
Skimmed Milk

LUNCH

1 cup of brown rice
1 cup of lettuce with tomatoes
(add a salad dressing of your choice)
Roasted chicken breast
Fruit juice or water

DINNER

1 cup of brown rice
Sautéed mixed vegetables
Steamed sausages
Water

TUESDAY

BREAKFAST

Two slices of wheat bread
(with your choice of spread)
Boiled egg
Coffee or cocoa drink

LUNCH

1 cup of brown rice
1 cup of lettuce with sliced apples
2 pieces of big beef patties
Fruit juice or water

DINNER

1 cup of brown rice
Spinach in garlic and oyster sauce
Buttered garlic shrimp
Water

WEDNESDAY

BREAKFAST

1/2 cup of fried rice
Sunny side up egg
Chorizo sausage
Coffee or cocoa

LUNCH

1 cup of wheat spaghetti in pesto sauce
1 cup of lettuce with small, sliced pears
Chicken strips
Fruit juice or water

DINNER

1 cup of brown rice
1 small bowl of vegetable soup with real cabbages
Pan-fried fish (dory)

THURSDAY

BREAKFAST

2 pcs of pancake
3 pcs of bacon
Low calorie maple syrup
Coffee or cocoa

LUNCH

1 cup of brown rice
Mussels with ginger soup
Sautéed mixed vegetables
Fruit juice or water

DINNER

1 cup of brown rice
Roasted pork in barbecue sauce
1 cup of spinach salad with your own choice of salad dressing

BREAKFAST

1 slice of sourdough wheat bread
Add avocado and egg on top
Coffee or cocoa

LUNCH

1 cup of brown rice
Sautéed French beans in oyster sauce
Fried chicken
Fruit juice or water

DINNER

1 cup of seafood pasta
1 cup of lettuce with mango
(and your own choice of salad dressing)
Any kind of seafood that goes well with your pasta

BREAKFAST

Fruit cereal with granola
1 sliced of wheat bread
Coffee or cocoa

LUNCH

1 cup of brown rice
Tuna with string beans
Steamed broccoli

DINNER

1 cup of brown rice
Sweet and sour fish
1 cup of lettuce with tomatoes
(and your choice of salad dressing)

BREAKFAST

Omelet with ham and cheese
Two slices of wheat bread
Coffee or cocoa

LUNCH

1 cup of brown rice
Your choice of fast food (yes, it's okay to eat fast food
once in a while)
Spinach salad and your choice of salad dressing

DINNER

1 cup of brown rice
Pan-fried buttered salmon
Steamed broccoli & carrots

Simple recipes and easy to follow, aren't they? You now have a simple healthy recipe for one week. Now let me explain some hidden secrets in the following meal plan.

Always look for these three whenever you have a meal: Carbohydrates, Protein and Greens. If your plate has all of these three — it could be anything of your choice — and you consume the right amount, you're on the right track.

Some other tips that can really simplify your healthy meal plans:

Always go WHEAT (wheat bread, brown rice, wheat pancake or anything that is will be rich in fiber).

Always go GREEN (salad, spinach, beans, broccoli, avocado. These are all superfoods and will definitely make you healthy).

Always go MEAT (make sure you consume some beef, pork, chicken and seafood. It will make you feel stronger and even improve your muscles). As you may have noticed, I didn't put an amount you have to consume under this category because I want you to make that choice for yourself. My point is that it's okay for the meat to fill up your stomach rather than rice.

However, if your preference is to avoid eating meat in your diet, you may ignore this tip.

As you may have noticed, I'm not sharing a strict diet plan to deprive you of something or to make you feel frustrated. This healthy meal plan aims for you to create healthy eating habits and expand your food choices. Moreover, there are other things that you must really keep in check when you want to follow the path of being healthy:

Reduce your sugar intake. Use zero calorie sugar for your coffee or drinks. Instead of eating 5 pieces of donuts, just eat one donut a day, until you can just eat one donut per week, or per month. The same goes for other desserts like cake, ice cream, milk tea and others. Take note: We still need sugar in our body, and it's still okay to eat sweets once in a while. You just have to know when enough is enough.

Once you're able to keep these pointers at the forefront of your mind, you will be just fine. I am not a professional dietician; I am merely sharing with you what I do and what I eat in order to stay healthy pre and post birth. I want to keep it real. I don't count all of my calories or go into calorie deficits since I'm still nursing my little one. I eat what I want and what I need. However, I know when it's too much and when it's enough. I try to regulate my intake of desserts, especially those sweet ones, as much as possible.

I suggest you discover your limitations and stop stress eating. You can get it done, Momshie, and it won't cost you time or your happiness. Be sensible and know your limits. You can do this! And please remember to consult your physician before engaging in any kind of diet or exercise plan.

Self-care Prescription
Fitness Routine

Being fit and staying fit are the things that we want to achieve when we become a mom — not only to lose the extra pounds we gained from pregnancy, but to also keep our bones and muscles strong for increased energy.

I am not a professional fitness trainer, but I am a fitness enthusiast and a mom. Hear when I say that it's possible. I manage to make it happen, and so can you!

Being fit does not mean being sexy like a model. It's not all about body shape and vanity. We all have to realize that fitness is all about making you feel better, making you feel confident, and making you feel stronger like a badass mom. You know it's true when you say the words, "Ah, I feel so much better," after sweating your ass off following a fitness routine. Release your endorphins, Momshies, by getting it done.

We are all busy moms, and we always want something quick and doable. What I'll be sharing with you are basic exercises that do not require any gym equipment except for a yoga mat. These exercises are what I do, and they will only consume little amounts of your time. However, you have to be consistent, committed and make it a part of your lifestyle.

REMINDER & DISCLAIMER

Reminder and Disclaimer: Consult your doctor before proceeding with any fitness routine, especially if you're still in your first-year, post birth.

One Minute Wall Sit (3 sets, total of 3 minutes)

Lean against any flat wall with your knees bent into a seated position while your feet are flat on the floor (yes, it's like sitting without a chair). Try to do this for one minute, if not, you can try doing it for 30 seconds.

You will definitely feel the burn on your legs while doing this exercise. That's okay. It means you're doing it right. This exercise also works your core.

Walking Lunges (3 sets, 6 repetition or reps on each side)

It's like walking but bending your right knee while stepping with your left leg straight, and vice versa.

Alternative for low impact: Standing Lunges. You have to bend your right knee while straightening your left leg, and vice versa. There is no need to step on it. This is perfect if you don't have enough space in your home or backyard to complete walking lunges.

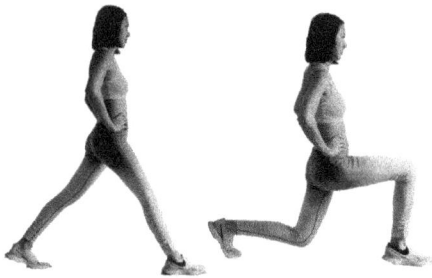

Curtsy Squats (3 sets, 6 reps each side)

Put your hands together and stand upright. Slowly get your body lower as if you're picking up something from the floor, and cross your left leg behind your right leg until your hips reach a squat position. Slowly stand up through your right leg and repeat vice versa. Make sure to maintain a face-forward position, and keep your chest out.

Bird Dog (3 sets, 6 reps each side)

Kneel on your mat with your hands firmly on the ground. When you feel steady and ready, point your arm straight out in front of you and extend the opposite leg behind. You should look like one straight line from your hand to your foot. Hold this position for a few seconds and return your hands and knees to the starting position. Do the same for the other side.

The challenge in doing this exercise is balance. You will get the hang of it and master your balance through practice.

DAY 2: ARMS & SHOULDERS
Arm Circles (3 sets, 15 circles each rotation)

Extend both arms out straight while standing comfortably with your feet firmly on the ground. Slowly rotate your shoulders and arms to make forward circles.

Boxing Punches (3 sets, 15 punches each side)

Create a fighting posture position to get ready to punch. Extend your arm across your body like you're punching an imaginary bag in front of you. Keep your focus and release a force with your punch, but be wary to not over-punch as it could overextend your shoulder muscles.

Triceps Dips (3 sets, 12 reps)

Look for a sturdy object in your home. This could be your chair, couch, coffee table or any strong platform that you can lean on to do this exercise. Place your hands shoulder-width apart on the couch. Extend your legs, with your pelvis shifted forward as a starting position. Slowly bend your legs with your feet firmly on the floor. Slowly and gently pull yourself up while bending your knee.

Caution: don't lock your knees.

Bicep Curls (3 sets, 12 reps)

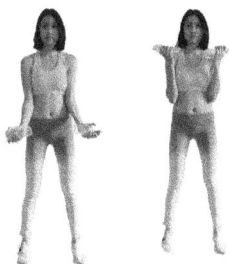

Start by looking for a bottle of water that you can hold in each of your hands. Position your elbow at your sides and your forearms should extend on the inside of your body. Bring the bottle of water all the way up to your shoulders by bending your elbows. Hold onto that position for three seconds while squeezing the muscle and reverse the curls slowly and repeat.

DAY 3: PARTIAL REST DAY

Engage in light cardio or movement. You can play your favorite sports on this day, like badminton, tennis or swimming. You can just go for a walk at the park or around your neighborhood to keep your muscles moving.

DAY 4: CHEST AND BACK

Superman (3 sets, 1 minute each set)

Lie on your stomach while extending your arms and legs out like a superman. Slowly lift your arms and legs simultaneously as high as you can. Hold this position for one minute, or for as long as possible (as long as you're comfortable in the position). Make sure to keep looking straight ahead to ensure good posture.

Cat Stretch (3 sets, 15 reps)

Imitate a dog position as a starting position. Take a deep breath. As you exhale, push your belly towards your spine, curving your back to the ceiling. Hold this position for three seconds, and then slowly bring your posture back to normal. Reminder: always tighten your core to maximize the effect of the exercise.

Push Ups (3 sets, 10 reps)

Get on the floor and start pushing up your body by extending your arms up and down gently and slowly (making sure that you remain comfortable).

Plank (3 sets, 1 minute each)

Get on the floor and extend your legs, resting your elbows on the ground. Hold your core and hold that position for one minute. This is honestly my favorite workout as it really burns the fat on my belly and strengthens my lower back, which is highly affected when you carry your little one too much.

DAY 5: CARDIO
It is all about keeping your heart rate racing and up. Go for a bike ride, swim or join a Zumba party.

DAY 6: REST DAY YOUR DAY OFF
Take time to focus on your mind, your family and friends.

DAY 7: STILL A PARTIAL REST DAY
Engage in a little bit of cardio, like walking and dancing to keep your muscles awake and moving.

IMPORTANT NOTES

- Always include STRETCHING before and after your workout.

- Always eat meals that are rich in protein right after you work out.

- You can have a sports massage when you deem it necessary. It's important to keep your blood circulation flowing.

- Treat your fitness journey as a part of your life. Make it a daily habit.

Now that it's all here, and you've been given a week of your workout schedule, it's your turn to decide if you will let yourself become fit and get started. Get it done, Momshie! You can do this!

CHAPTER 4

We all Feel Isolated at Times

It's a surprise that motherhood also often comes with the feeling of isolation and loneliness. However, it is actually fairly common for us to feel this way right after giving birth. It's like waking up one day and realizing that you're not the same person anymore who used to be able to do a lot of things, including socializing. Our world turns upside down when the little one arrives and, in turn, has transported us Momshies into a whole new world.

As a first time mom, I never knew that I'd feel so isolated from my friends and even my family. Also, knowing that none of my friends had started a family yet, created more unwanted isolation. The feeling of loneliness and isolation crept up on me, and I didn't feel like anyone could relate to me anymore. This is a slippery slope, Momshies, and when you begin to feel this way, my suggestion to you is to find someone to talk to right away. Loneliness can become a disaster, especially if you feel like no one understands you.

My life began to feel like it was stuck on repeat. Mom duties were being hurled at me from every direction. From previously working and traveling so much to now being a stay-at-home mom was an enormous transition. This also added to the isolation and loneliness I was feeling.

However, I chose to stop whining (in my mind) and focus instead on the fact that I had a happy, healthy baby whom I got to see every day. How lucky I was, and am, to witness all of his milestones! I painted a fake, tired smile on my face. I put a metaphorical shield and spear in my hand and acted as if I was the happiest and bravest mother in the whole wide world. This worked for a little while…

Until one night, I finally burst into tears and talked to my husband. I knew I needed to let it all out and share my feelings with somebody. I'm fortunate to have a partner in life who's willing to listen and is always there for me. After our deep and emotional conversation, he connected with me and understood the isolation, the shame and the loneliness I was feeling. He then urged me to make time for myself by doing what I love and pointed out the importance of having a 'life' outside motherhood. I realized that night, in my husband's caring arms, that it was so important to address our feelings and to do something about it.

The next day, I embarked on finding some help. I hired a nanny, a fitness instructor for my physical health, and I started learning how to drive a car. My most recent epiphany has been diving into a journey I never thought I'd be able to do — writing. And so my first book was born because I was given the space and time to be creative while I asked for help.

I've never been so joyful, or more grateful, as I am now taking care of my little one. It's really true that what you feel inside will resonate with your baby.

The bottom line is that if you're feeling isolated and lonely, there's no shame in accepting and embracing these feelings. We all need to put down our shield and start letting some people into our lives to listen and to help us through the day. We need to deal with it and start doing things we love and that motivate us, not only for our own sanity but also for the sake of our kids.

Upon having experienced this for myself, I have come up with some specific ways to help us feel less isolated and more involved with our life and community:

Reconnect with Yourself

Going through pregnancy and childbirth is both mind-blowing and overwhelming. Reconnecting with ourselves is vital in understanding how we can get through isolation or loneliness.

So how do you start reconnecting with yourself after so many long months and years?

MEDITATE

Close your eyes and remember the days you had before motherhood. Connect with your inner feelings and understand your emotions. Make it a habit to do this every day for at least three minutes. This can build your awareness and can help you bring back control into your life. By doing this, you will realize what you can do to reconnect with yourself. You may go back to a hobby that you used to do before motherhood, or you could start a new fitness journey. Whatever it is, do something new outside motherhood that fills your soul and makes you feel like your authentic self.

START WRITING A JOURNAL

I believe that 'writing is the best way to talk without being interrupted'. Writing down your thoughts, ideas and feelings will help you to stay connected with yourself in the wonderful yet complicated world of motherhood. Through writing, you might also realize the progress you're making, giving yourself an opportunity to celebrate small triumphs in order to feel involved and less lonely.

GO FOR A WALK

Take a short break from your kids, and take a walk whenever you can in a public park or even just in your backyard. It is nice to keep moving while thinking — it helps you to concentrate and think about yourself and the important things in life. Walking can alleviate your stress and help you feel relaxed while reconnecting with yourself. So, try to walk for at least 15 minutes outside your house, observe your surroundings, feel the air, notice the movement of the trees, take a deep breath and connect deeply with your inner self.

WEAR YOUR FAVORITE CLOTHES

This is just a small thing, but it could really give you back a sense of yourself. Some of your clothes might not fit just yet, and that's okay. Choose an old pair of jeans you want to get back into and label them your 'goal jeans'. In the meantime, choose the clothes you can currently fit into, and get up and dress up, Momshie! Take a moment to look at the dress you've worn before — perhaps one you wore on your first date with your husband. When you see that specific dress or outfit hanging in the closet, maybe a flood of memories will start to rush into your mind and give you that same giddy feeling that you felt when you were wearing that beautiful dress. Remember those romantic days? Feels familiar and it gives you comfort, doesn't it? This also works when you want to reconnect with yourself.

One of the reasons why I felt disconnected with myself when I got pregnant, and a few months after pregnancy, is the fact that I could no longer wear the favorite clothes that I used to wear.

Every time I looked in the mirror, I saw a completely different person. But when I started to lose my pregnancy belly and began to fit into some of my old favorite clothes, it actually gave me a familiar feeling of my old self. It may be a simple thing, but it really gave me pure joy to wear my favorite clothes again. It triggered something in my mind and, somehow, I recognized myself and remembered my old self. Try to do it every day just for fun, and it could lighten up your whole day.

Always Reach Out

I've shared my story with you at the beginning of this chapter, and I let you know that the one thing that helped me a lot was when I decided to reach out to my husband and share my problems.

I have a strong personality, and I'm obsessed with pushing myself to the limit before reaching out to others. I wanted to solve my own problems and not disturb other people with my own struggles and circumstances. I just wanted to maintain that pretentious superpower of strength in order to save my face and not be perceived as weak. I have always found it difficult to ask for help, even more so when society keeps telling us to be strong, independent women.

GO MOMSHIE LITTLE SECRET — **Over-empowering yourself can lead to severe disempowerment and isolation. So, be very careful with how far you are willing to push yourself without getting into dire consequences.**

I'm not against being independent and being strong, but when you become a mom, things happen. Struggles and challenges will be common, and there'll definitely be times that you have to reach out to other people for some help and advice.

There is no set schedule to reach out to others; it's all about the need to share your feelings. There are a lot of things throughout your journey of motherhood that you need to get out of your system to lessen the weight you're carrying. I'll tell you once again, *you are not supposed to face motherhood alone.*

However, you should also remember that people around you, even your husband, are not mind readers. They may understand some of your gestures or body language, but it is not as concrete as the words that have to come from you. You need to speak up and communicate when you reach out.

Here are some benefits when you stop making excuses and decide to reach out when you need to:

★ *You will be able to deal with your feelings and thoughts instead of ignoring or escaping from them. Reaching out to somebody and sharing your frustrations, as well as your joys, is such a huge step in taking responsibility for your feelings through clear communication. I can't tell you enough how much relief it will give you and how much weight you will feel lifted from your shoulders.*

★ *We all know the fact that once you become a mom your world becomes hectic. So we tend to let the day pass us by, hoping that all our worries and frustrations will fade away. The reality is that those feelings (whatever you're feeling right now) will drag you down and go on and on until you find yourself in the corner of your room crying and feeling alone. Do not wait for that moment, Momshie! Reach out whenever it's needed. Don't wait until it's too heavy before reaching out; deal with it right away. Don't wait until it's too late, and then you can avoid feeling really low.*

★ *A practical way of dealing with your thoughts and feelings is to set aside a few moments every day for yourself to choose what you will need to do in order to exercise self-care. It may be talking to your loved one before you sleep or in the morning with your partner. You could even talk to your best friend to tell them about your day — how it has been and how you felt throughout the day. Having these daily conversations will keep you and your emotions in check.*

From the day I reached out to my husband, we made it a habit to talk to each other before going to sleep, and we love our night conversations — it's our quality time to share what we've learned for the day and to chat about our joys and pains we experienced that day. By doing this, we become accountable to each other, and we have developed an even stronger and deeper connection with each other. It's such a comfort to be able to do this with the love of your life.

When you decide to reach out, suddenly you will feel that you're not alone; there's somebody listening whom you trust and love, especially when things get tough. By letting yourself be under the umbrella of others when it rains, you will automatically feel protected. There's nothing like a sense of belonging during difficult times.

I've always reached out to my mom whenever there's something I couldn't understand when it came to taking care of my little one. She immediately helps me out, and she even enlists the help of my aunties to make sure that I get all the support I'll ever need. Sometimes it takes a village to solve a problem, and I'm so grateful to get the support and security I need in order to get through some challenges of motherhood. You can also build your own village by reaching out to your trusted people.

You will gain countless benefits when you reach out. But are you brave enough? Yes, of course you are, Momshie! You are brave and you are important! It's a matter of changing your perspective and taking off your shield. Be prepared to let people into your wonderful, yet complicated, motherhood life.

Hang Out with Other Momshies (Online or Offline)

I've shared with you earlier that none of my closest friends have started a family yet, so knowing that I have nobody within my known circle of friends to reach out to, to ask about motherhood or even share my frustrations with, is hard. However, the internet has been a friend of mine for a while now, and being able to reach out to my distant friends or even colleagues on social media really helps me to share my journey of motherhood.

I have discussed the benefits of joining online communities in Chapter 1, but I just want to emphasize here once more how easy it is to reach out to these groups. In the advent of technology, different online and social apps have been created especially for moms. Talking to somebody has become much easier, and in just one click, or by finding the courage to join in on a group, you can now have access to different mom stories and struggles that you can probably relate to. The support you get from an online community can make you feel connected and safe. It also gives you different perspectives of motherhood that could help you make a few wiser decisions in life. There is power in numbers.

If you like taking the initiative, you may even start creating your own group online, or offline, by reaching out to all the moms you know in your area or selecting people from your list of Facebook friends. There's nothing wrong with starting small by bringing together all the moms around you. Always remember that moms have common ground; we all feel the same at one time or another.

Spend Some Time Out

This does not necessarily mean the 'Me Time' I've shared in Chapter 1, but it means taking time to go out of your house, with or without your little one.

One of the reasons why being a stay-at-home mom feels lonely sometimes is because we sometimes forget that we need to go out and get some fresh air. Being a stay-at-home mom doesn't mean that you have to stay locked up in your house all the time. There's nothing wrong with being a stay-at-home mom — my deepest respect goes out to all of you — but loneliness kicks in when you're at home and alone with your kids all the time. This is not healthy, Momshies, so planning trips to go outside to do errands, meet friends or just to do a little bit of shopping is important for your mental health and wellbeing.

We are human beings; we are born to socialize and explore. Have you noticed your baby? They're the most socialized human beings in the world! They love to interact with people by smiling, cooing, blabbing and even laughing…it's like music to my ears. They also love to play with babies who are the same age as them. They feel lonely when they are kept inside with nobody to play with, and it's the same with us. We feel lonely because we do the same things over and over again, and we're too busy making our house a home. Find the time to go out, and travel if you can.

I have mentioned in previous chapters that I gave birth during the outbreak of the COVID-19 pandemic, and strict restrictions on travelling were being implemented. I became sick to my stomach every time I had to risk going outside of the house. We would go for a short stroll down our street in his pram, and go for checkups with his pediatrician, but that was it. My social life went from meeting new people on a daily basis, and visiting new venues, to almost zero meetings and outings. Only a few friends were able to visit me and my baby at home due to the fear of possibly bringing the virus with them.

The bottom line is that I have felt very isolated and lonely in these unprecedented times, but I always made sure to spend some time outside of the house, even just to wave at neighbors over the fence. You will be amazed how a smile or a wave from people other than your family can also make your day.

So, Momshie, if you're reading this and you have the freedom to go out with your kids, travel to the beach, go to different countries or even just eat at restaurants. Go for it! If you have the chance to meet other people wherever you go and enjoy your kids' school programs and events by being there, go for it! If you can just go to the park full of other kids who are playing, let your kids play and enjoy the trees! If you can spend time outside with your mom friends, even for an hour or two, go for it! If you just want to spend your time hiking or jogging on a mountain, go for it!

Having experienced being stuck at home during the pandemic, it made me realize the things we took for granted whenever we were outside the house before the virus came. My motherhood journey would have been so much better, I guess, without the pandemic. But, I still wouldn't trade all the experiences I've gained and the memories I've had while spending time with my little one at home every single day during these trying times. I am fortunate enough to have my whole family living under the same roof as me and my baby. We have bonded and had time to watch Seiya grow with an immaculate support system around him.

There are so many benefits you can get from spending time outside of your house. Not only does it improve your physical health, but it also improves your mental health, and it reduces stress, anxiety and loneliness.

So if you're feeling isolated or lonely, I want you to know, Momshies, that it's okay. We all experience this, and we can all get through this. You may be in a more difficult situation, but always remember that somebody will be there for you. Open your arms and hearts, and let people come into your life.

QUESTIONS TO PONDER

List down some reasons why you feel isolated and lonely

_____

_____

_____

_____

_____

_____

_____

_____

_____

_____

_____

_____

_____

_____

Write down the names of trustworthy friends, community platforms and family members who you can reach out to

_____

_____

_____

_____

_____

_____

_____

_____

_____

_____

_____

_____

_____

_____

_____

_____

_____

How do you describe yourself?

_____

_____

_____

_____

_____

_____

_____

_____

_____

_____

_____

_____

_____

_____

_____

_____

Write down all of the places you would like to visit

_____

_____

_____

_____

_____

_____

_____

_____

_____

_____

_____

_____

_____

_____

_____

_____

_____

_____

READ THIS OUT LOUD & REPEAT IT UNTIL YOU FEEL IT

Reaching out to people and asking for support will help me feel a sense of belonging that could help me obtain the warm embrace I need to get through some rainy days in my life. I shall try harder to reconnect with myself every day in order to find myself again. I will commit to becoming a better version of my old self and, most importantly, to be a better mom.

_____

Signature & Date

CHAPTER 5

We Struggle in Silence

"*Am I a bad mom because I chose to continue working rather than spending time with my kids at home?*"

"*Am I a bad mom just because I took a longer shower yesterday?*"

"*Am I a bad mom just because I missed the first word and first step of my baby?*"

"*Am I a bad mom just because I spent Friday night with my friends?*"

"*Am I a bad mom because I train so hard as an athlete that I rarely have time with my baby?*"

Sound familiar? We all struggle in silence, and we all feel the same thing. But hell no, you are not a bad mom.

We all had our hobbies, careers, businesses or something that we did to help create our identity, but all of these hobbies and habits were set aside initially as we took up the role of becoming a mother.

Motherhood is a long journey, and it's never-ending. Let's all be honest here, Momshies. Maybe you've felt it before, or you're feeling it now, or maybe not yet, but there'll be a point in your life that you will crave to do something for yourselves; to continue what we had before motherhood or to start reviving the dreams we always wanted to pursue and achieve other than motherhood. I'm telling you there's nothing wrong with all of these. There's nothing wrong with going back to work, or doing things for ourselves and drinking warm coffee in the morning. However, society keeps on telling us what a mother should and shouldn't do, and this causes too many high expectations which makes 'mom guilt' even stronger.

What is 'mom guilt' anyway?

It's guilt that you feel when you think that you're not enough as a parent or that you're not doing the right things for your little one. It is also a relentless struggle with your conscience when you do something for yourself over your duties as a mom. It is super real, and if it's not already happening, it will be knocking at your door soon enough.

Mom guilt exists for working moms, but also for stay-at-home moms. Some questions that may be brewing in your mind might be:

"Am I cooking enough great and healthy meals?"

"Are my kids having too much screen-time?"

"Is my house clean?"

"Am I buying enough educational toys for my baby?"

"Am I bonding with my baby properly?"

"Am I lacking patience with, and understanding of, my kids?"

"Is it my fault?"

"I'm a bad mom because my baby is not as chunky as other babies of the same age."

There will be so many times you will feel like you've screwed up, that you've failed and you're not good enough. Remember that in the eyes of your child, you are a super mom, and in the eyes of your partner, you're a warrior and the love of their life.

Let me tell you how this mom guilt kept rearing its ugly head in my life as a mom.

Since my little one was born, I had been a hands-on mom. I always made sure that everything was in order and well researched before doing something for my baby. For the first few weeks after my baby arrived, I recalled that even going to the bathroom was hard for me. I would hear cries in my head, so I would rush back to him like a frantic person, sometimes not even finishing my business in the bathroom. I also recalled setting my alarm for just 30 minutes or an hour because I didn't want my baby to miss me, but really I just didn't want to feel like I was neglecting him by prioritizing myself.

I would also have those moments when I couldn't continue working or do other things because I'd feel like I was a bad mother if I chose work over my mom duties. I also hesitated to spend dinners and coffee breaks with my husband because I thought it was unfair to leave my baby behind.

This guilt had been creeping around in my mind and heart, and it was an awful feeling and so confusing. I have been told that feeling this way is very normal, because your new baby is so vulnerable. But let me tell you something, feeling guilt is not a normal emotion. You are perfect the way you are, Momshie, and you definitely need time to focus on yourself and take time to look after your needs.

I suddenly had an awakening when I realized that nobody was telling me to take a quick shower or even sleep as little as possible. Nobody ever blatantly said to me, "Shame on you," when I was working, doing my fitness routine or spending time with my husband. I was, in essence, doing all of this to myself. It was all in my head; I was beating myself up because of the power of guilt.

Society has played a pivotal role in helping us judge each other, and it has assisted in putting guilt on us to become the 'ideal mom'. Let me tell you something, Momshies: the 'ideal mom' persona is in our heads, so when we fail to be what society is trying to tell us to become, we fall into the mom guilt trap and it takes a lot of time, courage and endurance to escape from it. It is a powerful and debilitating emotion that can literally push you to do things out of the ordinary.

Working moms tend to buy more things, and even expensive things, that aren't really necessary for their kids to make up for the time they've missed. Some moms tend to cover their guilt by tidying up the house, fixing some furniture they don't really need to fix and buying extra items for the house. These are just some ordinary ways of covering our guilt.

For some moms, the guilt pushes them to run away from their house; to divert their guilt by doing some impulsive things like piercing their nipple, getting a tattoo, smoking weed and dying their hair with unusual colors. Some of them cry every night, although they pretend to be happy in front of people.

These are examples of different moms I have encountered who have different ways of covering up the guilt. The bottom line is that if we let mom guilt get to us, it can turn our world upside down. It can drive us crazy and encourage us to do things we really don't mean.

So I decided to research some solutions that could help me overcome my mom's guilt. I found out that the guilt is going to be with me forever — it's forever a part of me. Sounds terrifying, doesn't it? On the plus side, there's a little bit of goodness in guilt as it helps us keep ourselves in check. We just have to learn to keep it at a manageable level.

Include Yourself

We tend to remove ourselves from the equation all the time when we do something in our daily life. When we do certain things, we do them mainly for our family, our loved ones. They are the reason why we do things. We prioritize the welfare of our family, and that's completely okay. But, try to think about when you did something that was solely for you and not your family.

Momshie, YOU MATTER! You need to become your reason why. This is important. Actually, it is the most important aspect of alleviating mom guilt. You have to put yourself at the forefront of your life. You won't feel the guilt if you understand that your happiness also matters. So you should do some things outside of motherhood that make you happy. The message remains the same. Go Momshie! Just do it!

Some scenarios to ponder that might help you realize the importance of including yourself

a. I will just stay at home just to prove to everyone that I'm a good mom.

   Include yourself: I will continue working as I've worked all my life for my dream job and to help support my family's finances and leisure. This also gives me self-satisfaction and motivation to create a family. I want what works for me, my baby and my partner. I'm a good mom because I am able to provide for my family while loving them with all my heart.

b. I will just cook all the time for the family even though I'm beyond exhausted.

   Include yourself: I am tired and stressed out. I will just order pizza for dinner so I can relax even for a little while. My time also matters. Everybody enjoys pizza so it's okay.

I'm still a good mom because I thought about pizza for dinner rather than serving nothing at all.

c. I will just continue breastfeeding even if it hurts and I struggle with my time and my work.

Include yourself: I will discontinue breastfeeding because it hurts me, and I can't function well as a person. I also have to stop so I can work properly in the office without the need of pumping in the storage room all the time. Giving formula to my baby does not make me less of a mom. It exists for a reason.

d. I will clean the house so my partner is happy when he gets home and my baby is always neat and clean.

Include yourself: When I'm exhausted, I'll just let the house get messy in order to make some time for myself. Sometimes, doing something random like browsing our family album rather than cleaning the house is okay. My decisions do matter, and taking my time to slow down and reflect also matters.

e. I will make sure to prepare my baby's food and be as creative and healthy as possible.

Include yourself: It's okay to feed my little one ready-to-feed baby cereals and food that I can make in my own way. I am content with my cooking skills as a mom. I am enough.

It's good to include yourself in the equation, isn't it? It feels good to know that you have a choice, and you're free to make your motherhood journey your way. If you include yourself in the equation, there will be less mom guilt because you know your WHY and that what you do works for you and your family.

The bottom line is that you need to begin to look at your reflection in the mirror and remind yourself that you're enough — what you do matters, what you feel matters and your choices in life matter.

Say No To Bragging Rights

There are a lot of moms in this world. Millions? Billions? Trillions? The count goes on. There are also a lot of mom communities around the world, online and offline. As mentioned earlier, social media has become a platform for moms; somewhere they can share everything about their babies — both the struggles and the celebrations. It's also become a platform for comparing and judging each other, neither of which is necessarily helpful in this complicated world called motherhood.

Comparing your baby to other babies is a HUGE NO. And I know you hate it when people do it to you. When you negatively compare your motherhood style with somebody else's, you're just beating yourself up for no reason and doing a huge disservice to yourself. They say, don't compare a pomelo to an orange. Even though they're both part of the citrus family, they're still different, so it's just wrong to compare.

Comparing yourself to others will not only create more doubt about yourself, it will also distract you from your goals as a mom. It's also a fast track to unhappiness and guilt traps.

But with the internet ruling the world, it's really hard to ignore pictures and videos of other moms. They seem to look happier, wealthier, healthier and more successful, thus you can't help but compare yourself, which certainly makes your mom's guilt even stronger. The answers to avoiding this, lie in what you can do when you're tempted to compare yourself with other moms.

GO🪷
MOMSHIE
LITTLE SECRET

Count. Your. Blessings. It's easy to find goodness in other people's lives, yet we tend to ignore some of the greatest blessings in our own lives. When we are focused on somebody else's victories, we forget to cherish our own. Counting your blessings isn't a cliché, but it's a good reminder for us to look at the small stuff, and be grateful for what we have.

It is important to appreciate our life even more once we are moms; to feel content and to look at our life in a brighter and more positive way. It's also nice to be reminded that, for sure, someone somewhere is dreaming of having what you have, so be even more grateful and appreciative of your life.

Once you've counted your blessings, you'll stop comparing yourself to others and will begin to focus on your own victories. Once you do that, you'll feel more accomplished as a mom and you will stop doubting yourself.

A mom who's suffering guilt
I'm a bad mom because I only fed my baby a ready-made cereal today.

A mom who's counted her blessings
I'm blessed to have the ability to feed my baby. And yay! He's full and healthy today.

A mom who's suffering guilt
I'm breastfeeding my baby only up to three months, but other moms breastfeed their babies for two years. I feel horrible as a mom.

A mom who's counted her blessings
I am thankful that I'm able to breastfeed my baby for three months,

and I'm blessed to provide him with formula which also helps my baby grow into a healthy and happy human.

Accept your imperfections. We are all far from being perfect, but we still tend to compare ourselves to others by looking at our imperfections. It is really important that we accept our weaknesses and imperfections in order to overcome jealousy and insecurity. It is this that leads to us comparing ourselves with other people.

Being perfect does not give you 'the most perfect mom medal award' and, most importantly, it won't help you solve and overcome mom's guilt. However, embracing your flaws, quirks and your imperfections will make you a better mom because you'll understand things better and feel lighter. So free yourself from comparisons, and start embracing your perfectly imperfect life. Don't be so serious, Momshies. Life is meant to be enjoyed.

Bragging is discouraged in the sphere of motherhood. Whoever brags about how good they are as a mother is probably nurturing mom guilt, and this can paint a rather isolated picture for those who become victims of bragging rights.

Let me tell you something. If you feel like you're doing better than other moms, it's okay, but letting other moms feel that you're better than them is not helpful at all. It's downright disrespectful. I know I sound like a broken record, but there's no prize for a mom who's better than others. Also, we all have to realize that being 'a good mom' is subjective. As far as I know, all of us are good moms in our own perfectly imperfect ways.

So please say no to bragging rights. You can share and inspire, but never ever let the intention be to brag. It does not achieve anything. In the end, the bragger ends up looking like a fool. Let's help each other by lifting each other up and complimenting one another, which indeed fosters a sense of community and oneness with others.

Value Your Intentions

All moms want the best for their children. All moms love their children despite the challenges that life throws at us.

GO@
MOMSHIE
LITTLE SECRET

Your intention as a mom is important. It all comes down to what's in your heart and what you desire. When you value your intention, you notice the process rather than the end product. For example, you may be late to your child's soccer game, but your intention is to be on time and witness your child's first goal. When you value your intention, the guilt of being late and missing some parts of the game won't matter anymore.

Let me reiterate this. We must focus on the process and not on the end product. We may not be the perfect mom, but we are doing things the best way that we can, and we are doing things for our kids out of love — that's what's important. You may be working very hard in your office so you feel like you're lacking as a mom, but you have to remind yourself that working hard is also a way of showing love for your kids and for your family. And you're doing that to prepare your kids for the future; to support your kids and their needs in the future, like their education and items that they need as they grow older.

Another very good example is this:

The first mom offers formula milk to her baby after birth, and the second mom offers breast milk to her baby after birth. They may have different ways of feeding their baby, but their intention is the same — to feed their baby and to make sure that that their baby will grow up healthy. They both love their babies regardless of the choices they make as mothers.

So ask yourself, Momshie, what your intention is whenever you prepare food for your baby. What is your intention whenever you work late at night? Whatever it is that you do, I'm sure that your intention is good for your baby. So keep doing what you think works for you. Reduce the mom guilt and focus on your heart, your intention and your goal as a mom.

WORKSHEETS TO WORK THROUGH YOUR GUILT

List down the reasons why you think you're NOT good enough as a mom:

_____

_____

_____

_____

_____

_____

_____

_____

_____

_____

_____

What do you do when mom guilt kicks in? (It's okay to write some of the crazy things that you do! And be completely honest with yourself. These worksheets are to help with INTENTION.)

_____

_____

_____

_____

_____

_____

_____

_____

_____

_____

_____

_____

_____

_____

_____

Give some credit to yourself. What are the things that you do for your baby or family that make you proud and happy?

_____

_____

_____

_____

_____

_____

_____

_____

_____

_____

_____

_____

_____

_____

_____

_____

_____

_____

_____

_____

_____

_____

_____

_____

_____

_____

READ & REPEAT IT UNTIL YOU FEEL IT

I understand my worth, my intentions and my own situation. I feel more grateful when I start to count my blessings and when I stop comparing myself to other moms. I'm trying to understand now that my life situation and circumstances are unique, and so is my motherhood style. I shall continue to keep love as my intention in doing things for my kids and family. I shall also remember, at all times, to include myself in the equation because I matter.

_____

Signature & Date

THE GIFT OF WRITING

GO MOMSHIE
LITTLE SECRET

The next chapter is a part of my giveaway to you, Momshies, to show you that one of my dreams was to be a published author and, well, here we are! You are holding my book in your hands and reading some suggestions that got me to where I am today. Once I alleviated my own mom guilt, I realized that one of my dreams was to write.

Writing has been my best friend, especially during tough times. It started when I was in college. A friend told me to create my own writing website using a free platform online to publish my essays and school work since he saw the potential in me. I felt encouraged, and I started my own writing on my website. However, I never posted any school work or boring essays on there. Instead, I wrote and published anything that bothered me. In short, I wrote when I was sad or confused about something, especially when a topic affected me personally.

When I became a mom, a lot of things changed, and honestly I was not always happy and ready to go into the battlefield. Thus I started writing and pouring my heart out, hoping that I'd get the comfort, the wisdom and the answers I was looking for.

It worked. This book definitely paved the way to my deepest realization as a first-time mom. And I wish, from the bottom of my heart, to share with you the magnificent and positive effect of writing and journaling.

Writing has a purpose, and it has the power to transform you like it did for me.

We all have a story to tell, and the next pages offer you some space TO WRITE YOUR OWN STORY.

I would like to collect some stories from Momshies all over the world, so we can collaborate one day and possibly create a book together. If you feel so inclined, please write your story and send it to me at: gomomshie@gmail.com. I can't wait to hear from you.

CHAPTER 6

Working Moms

The present moment is all we have, and I would like to dedicate this chapter to all the working moms out there.

Being a mom is already hard enough; building a career is nearly impossible, especially if you're a new mom. But you're a badass, and I know you've got this, Momshies!

If you're working because you don't have a choice, this is for you. If you're working because it is your passion and it's a part of who you are, then this chapter is also for you.

No judgment here, but some of us need to work for a living to put food on the table, and sometimes we can feel like there is no respite. At the end of the day, our title of 'mom' is no doubt the most important role we have when we take on the amazing task of motherhood.

When I was young, I told myself, 'I will work no matter what happens, even while being a mom. I will because I want to, and I will financially provide for my family because I can."

These words percolated in my mind as early as thirteen years of age because I witnessed what my mom had to endure when I was growing up. She didn't have the chance to work. Her generation encouraged women to stay at home and focus on their children and their husbands despite circumstances and financial shortcomings. Here we are now, in 2021, living in a modern day society where the rules change every day. Women now have the choice and freedom to work and provide for their families. Change is good, and I love having a free spirit. As I write this, I feel empowered!

However, when I became a mom for the first time and stayed at home for months taking care of my baby, I almost gave up on my vision of building a career while being a mom. I tried to start a business or even to start some small online jobs, but the pressure of society got to me, and I just suddenly felt that if I continued working, I was prioritizing my needs over my baby's. It seemed so wrong at that time. I felt discouraged and unmotivated. But then one night, I talked to my husband and confessed to him that it felt impossible to do both things at the same time. I also didn't see the purpose of why I kept pushing my career while I had just become a mother. I thought that maybe it was best to give myself time to breathe and focus on my new role as a mom. His words will forever stay in my mind.

"I know you as a restless and ambitious person, even before our baby arrived. I see that you're already trying to do multiple things at the same time when you're still in the phase of discovering yourself, so don't stop. Being a mom may be hard, but don't let it hinder you from discovering yourself and your true potential. Don't ever think that you're neglecting our baby's needs just because you try to build your own career. Remember that you're doing that because you also want to be a role model for our kids in the future. You are a strong and independent woman, and our kids will know and admire you for who you are when they can see you multitasking and doing what makes you happy."

When I heard him say these words, I realized that I had forgotten who I was. It's true that sometimes we need somebody to remind us of who we used to be, before we gain our new title of 'mom'. As a new mom, we tend to submerge ourselves so far into this role that we forget who we are or where we were. I'm beyond grateful that I have a supportive husband who knows me deeply and understands me. He hears me while always providing great insights into what I have accomplished in my life. So this was the moment I decided NOT to stop, and I continued being who I always was. I began to build a career. I found out that juggling both a career and motherhood is possible, but I'll never tell you that it will be easy.

Let's be honest here. Working while having a child at home is a real struggle, and it will never ever be smooth sailing all the time. There are so many things that we juggle around in order to pursue a career while being a mom. Plus we also have a lot of underlying emotions when we go to work. Thinking about the situation of a working mom reminds me of how I truly appreciate single working moms out there who work to provide for the family. I still honestly don't know how you do it, Momshie, but you rock! Double hands down to you.

After giving birth, and making a commitment to go back to work, it can sometimes feel daunting. Most of us feel sad and lost. We're not a hundred percent sure that we want to be in the office; we feel like a part of us wants to stay at home because we don't want to miss out on some our baby's important milestones, and we don't want to be labelled a 'bad mom' just because somebody else is taking care of our baby during the day or during working hours.

Yet a part of us wants to go back to our office to create a life outside of motherhood, or to simply be able to financially provide for the family. But whatever your reasons, it won't change the fact that it's a real struggle to manage our emotions. On the other hand, if we know that our family is relying on us, we have to bite the bullet and do what we need to do in order to provide, regardless of our situation, and that's the true spirit of a working mom.

Imagine yourself, working 9 to 5 in an office and then when you get home, it's duty time with your little one right away. Imagine if you didn't even have time to decompress right after work, and you just had to get right back into your mom duties. Your lack of self-care would drop a hundred-fold. Creating a healthy balance for yourself and your baby is paramount in ensuring that you don't overwork yourself.

Each mom has different techniques to help her cope with life after maternity leave. Some moms handle it well like nothing has ever changed in them, but some take a while to go through the changes. Some moms feel like a new, empowered person, but some may feel lost. Whichever one of these moms you resonate with, know that it is okay and it's normal to feel either way. It is important to remember that you're not alone in this ongoing battle. There are billions of moms out there who have managed to do both and become successful.

In this chapter, let's discuss some tips that could help to uplift working moms.

Make It A Habit to Schedule Your Day

How can you balance your life and work? The answer is simple: SCHEDULING.

Scheduling will help you to be efficient in your role as a mom, wife, daughter, sister, friend, an employee, or as a CEO. It is important at the end of the day that we are still able to spend some quality time with our family despite our hectic lifestyle.

On some days it will seem like there aren't enough hours in a day to accommodate the things you have to do and want to do. You can start scheduling, a month or a week ahead, so you won't waste any precious time. This also means getting organized with everything, including planning out what you are going to wear the next day so you are not wasting time. You may use a color- coded Google calendar to help you be more organized. It's a useful tool, especially if you always use your phone or your computer to work on. If not, a planner or notebook is handy as well to create a schedule for you and your family.

GO
MOMSHIE
LITTLE SECRET

Priority comes along with scheduling. As a busy mom, it's necessary that we know how to remove some things from our life. We have to understand our priorities, and set aside things that you know don't help you or things that will make your day harder. This also includes choosing projects at work, and scheduling nights out with friends or meetings with family members. You can't accept all invitations. Scheduling also helps to set your boundaries and to limit yourself from unnecessary distractions in life. Once you know your priorities, you will wake up every morning driven and directed to the path that will make you productive and happy as a working mom.

You may also try to devise a family calendar if you have older kids. Then you all know when to make time for each other when things get too busy. It's nice to put it up in a living area or kitchen area so that everyone can see it and write on it whenever they can. This way, you will have a bird's eye view of what everyone has on their mind, and you will teach your kids firstly about scheduling, and then about compromise.

As a reward, scheduling will also give you time for yourself. Remember that self-care is so important. So, try your very best to stick with your schedule, Momshies.

Let It Go

There are a lot of things that hold us back from working, or even functioning, as a human being. So I'm going to say it again. LET IT GO.

Let go of the GUILT. It won't help you in any way. As I have stated and shared in the previous chapter, mom's guilt will just eat you alive. It can make you go crazy and it can cause you to run away from your home or even from yourself, which is the worst feeling in the world. You will feel defeated.

When you're at work, don't feel bad that you're not at home; instead make sure to be a hundred percent present when you *are* around your baby. Always relish and enjoy what's in front of you. I'll just remind you once again, being away from your child doesn't make you a bad mom.

Let go of YOURSELF. Too much attachment to your baby will just be harder for you to let go. This may not be the sweetest tip I can give you, but I want you to be firm with your decision and actions. If you have to go to work, let go of house chores and baby duties just for a little while. Be firm and move ahead so you can concentrate and be productive with your work. When you say goodbye to your baby when you leave for work, don't engage in long, drawn out moments because the baby will cling on to you and will eventually cry for longer from severe separation anxiety. Simply say goodbye and reassure your baby that you will be home soon. Don't make a big drama about leaving the house, because your baby will feel anxiety.

The bottom line here is to learn how to let go of expectations and responsibilities.

Forget About House Chores

In my opinion, these are things that are not a valuable use of your precious time, and these can be delegated to other people.

There are already apps available nowadays that allow you to book an affordable service to help clean up your house and do errands for you. So, if you don't have the time, or you don't want to do it, it's okay. Find someone else to clean your house. It's really not a big deal, Momshies. If this means that you can save some time and energy, and you can hold back on another kind of luxury, my suggestion would be for you to invest in some help.

I love to see my house clean. It honestly stresses me out when the house is a mess, but I hate doing the house chores and I'm not so skilled when I do it. So I decided to hire somebody else to do it for me weekly, and I am more than satisfied with the cleanliness of my home. Plus, I appreciate that I have more time to be with my baby and less time to worry about dirty dishes or a wrinkled shirt.

So, Momshie, make use of your time by doing the things that you love the most.

Always Remind Yourself of the Purpose

We might wake up one day and doubt the things we're doing in our life. It's like waking up on the wrong side of the bed, and suddenly we feel lost and uncertain about the decisions we have made recently. It might feel wrong that we're working as a mom because we're missing too much in our child's life. We might feel confused and doubtful. If all of these happen to you, always powerfully remind yourself of your purpose — why you've decided to be a working mom in the first place.

Purpose can be anything. It can be to put food on your table. It can be to attain financial freedom for your family, or it can be to attain something in your life that gives you happiness and contentment. Whatever your purpose is, you have to instill it in your mind or write it down in your notebook. Then, if bad days arrive, you have something to remind you of your purpose.

So, ask yourself and be certain about the purpose of your job. That is something you can use as a metaphorical spear and shield when the storms arrive.

Embrace the Separation Anxiety

One of the struggles we have as working moms is that it is natural to miss our babies when they are not near us. You know what's the good news? You can give in to the separation feeling and deal with it by indulging in new and innovative ways to stay connected with your kids even when you're far away.

Whenever you miss your kids or your husband during the day, embrace that feeling and allow yourself to alleviate that anxiety by having a video call with them. Or you could send your family pictures or messages online. This is a great way to ease your mind and your emotions, and it will then help you focus on work while feeling connected with your family. This is also possible even when you have a young baby at home. Of course, a baby can't read or use technology yet, but a nanny can send you a picture of your baby once in a while, or a message update throughout the day, to help you stay connected.

You may think that this contradicts the notion of 'let it go' which is stated above, but let me clarify this; letting go does not completely mean ignoring all your feelings and putting them to the side. Can you imagine working in the office and trying to fight the feeling of loneliness inside you? It's disturbing, right? As a matter of fact, fighting against your feelings of separation will only give you a harder time. So, forgive yourself, and walk at a slow pace. Give in to the separation anxiety until you're ready to be able to let go while you're at work.

Nobody Can Replace You

Most of us are afraid to let go of our guilt and ourselves because of the fear of being replaced as a mom. Stop the competition.

Stop the worries. Nobody's trying to take over your role as a mom even if you're spending long hours at work. Nobody can take your rights away as a mom, and nobody can ever replace you as a mom. Please don't ever forget that.

Be confident that you are enough, and believe that your love for your family is greater than anything in this world. You do you, Momshie!

WORKSHEETS FOR THE WORKING MOMSHIE

List down the emotions you feel when you're at work

_____

_____

_____

_____

_____

_____

_____

_____

_____

_____

_____

_____

List down all your frustrations as a working mom

_____

_____

_____

_____

_____

_____

_____

_____

_____

_____

_____

_____

_____

_____

_____

_____

_____

Think about your life. Look around you. What makes you feel like a badass?

_____

_____

_____

_____

_____

_____

_____

_____

_____

_____

_____

_____

_____

_____

_____

_____

_____

_____

What efforts will you engage in to balance your life at work and at home?

_____

_____

_____

_____

_____

_____

_____

_____

_____

_____

_____

_____

_____

_____

_____

_____

_____

Do this activity in order to release your thoughts and feelings of how you are as a working mom

_____

_____

_____

_____

_____

_____

_____

_____

_____

_____

_____

_____

_____

_____

_____

_____

_____

Use this space to draw or doodle anything that could symbolize your feelings as a working mom. Write your explanation as to why that particular object represents your emotions.

CHAPTER 7

We are Not JUST 'a Mom'

I might sound like a broken record, but let me tell you once again — working moms and stay-at-home moms are both extremely hard working and valuable members of our society. It is a choice that you have to make, and the most important thing is to make you happy so that everyone around you can feel your joy too.

If you're reading this and you feel unsure if you want to be a SAHM (stay-at-home mom) or not, I want you to know that it's common to have your doubts and fears. But never worry that it's because you don't love your children. I think rather it's because you may be scared to lose your identity. Don't think like that; no matter what you decide to do when your baby arrives, know that whatever you choose — whether to stay at home or go to work — know that you are making the best decision for your growth as well as for the future of your family.

I want to dedicate this chapter to all the stay-at-home Momshies out there, and share some interesting stories and thoughts about how a SAHM's life can be.

Let me just get this out now, let's all stop judging SAHMs. Let's stop the stigma surrounding the role of SAHMs and, most importantly, never look down on SAHMs. This may be harsh, but **shame on you if you do!**

You may think that it is an easy luxury; a privilege to stay at home without worrying about making money. Or maybe you consider that it's not 'real work' and everybody can do it. I have to stop you right there, right now, and I have to ask you to wake up and remove all these stigmas from your mind. All of these judgments are false.

SAHMs are the queens of their own castles — a homemaker, a house manager and a chief home officer. All that I've mentioned are highly ranked positions that deserve all the credit in the world. However, in reality, they don't receive *enough* credit. That's why I'm writing this chapter, so that everybody can relate to the reality of what stay-at-home moms have to endure.

My mom was a full-time SAHM, and I saw her engage in hard work around the house when I was growing up. However, when I was young I used to ask my mom, "Why aren't you at the office like my aunties?" Her reason was always that she had to stay at home to take care of us. She remained a firm believer of the saying, "It's better to take care of your own kids than let somebody else do it." Women of her generation were not encouraged to go to work, and they were expected to be home makers.

When my father passed away, Mom didn't have any other choice but to move into my aunt's house and take care of her home on a full-time basis while my family was staying there. It was an economical choice, because she couldn't afford to do much for us after my father passed on. As a single mom, with a huge disadvantage of not being a part of the workforce, the only choice for her was to stay at home and rely on her family's support. She may not have brought home a paycheck, or provided financial support for all of us, but the care and the love she exuded all day and every minute she was with us were definitely priceless.

I'm not proud to share experiences of when we did take our mom for granted, and I have felt and witnessed her sacrifices for us. There were moments when my siblings and I judged her and her duties as a mom. We complained about the house being a mess, about dirty clothes and about the food. Little did we realize how much work and effort she put into these tasks and, at the end of the day, even though she was tired, she still did what she needed to do to keep us happy, healthy and safe.

I wish I'd realized how hard I was on my mom when I was complaining about these small things. I am who I am today because my mom was a SAHM, and she provided for us in a different way. Not everything is about money all of the time. Her unwavering strength and love for me made me the woman I am today. I want to thank all of the moms who didn't really have a choice except to stay at home and look after their children. You are the unsung heroes of your generation. Thank you!

I became more appreciative of the life my mom had as a SAHM when I started staying at home after my own son was born. Everybody was quarantined or in lockdown due to COVID-19, and it was in this space that I realized the work she actually did for my siblings and I when she took care of us since birth. It is a lot harder than everyone thinks! From making sure that everybody had something to drink and eat at the table, to fixing our clothes for us so that we looked nice and presentable. From listening to our stories that she couldn't even relate to but she still tried so that we felt comfort and support, to just being around the house so she could be there to help us throughout the day. I can't describe how much comfort these little things brought to our life. Knowing that she was always around was very nurturing.

She was, and still is, literally a supermom. I have three other siblings, and she managed to raise us all being a SAHM. She even had twins, and my twin brother and I can't imagine how she managed to take care of us when we were little ones. Having a baby of my own made me realize how much time, effort and work it takes to care for a tiny human being. I applaud my mom for her patience and for *slaying* while staying at home like a queen.

How do SAHMs really feel?

Staying at home is a different kind of work. Some women find it easy, but some find it otherwise. We have to be real here. It's work that requires 24/7 of your time with no pay and, more often than not, with huge lack of sleep. Overall, it's a blessing and a choice we make out of love for our family. Like any other work, you have some good and some bad days, but a lot of SAHMs' struggles are not brought into the crowd because, mostly, they are the last people to speak up about needing help.

But here's the truth. SAHMs feel lonely. A mom whose life revolves around her children tends to forget her own needs. She becomes so busy tending to her kids' needs that she forgets how to go out and have fun with her friends without bringing the kids along. It's also one of the reasons why postpartum depression is most common amongst SAHMs.

SAHMs are discriminated against. This is the worst of it all. Society looks down on them simply because they don't bring home a paycheck and they're not living as a modern woman. They receive a lot of questions or comments like, "What do you do all day?", and, "It must be easy to be at home." As a result, almost all SAHMs lose their confidence and self-esteem because of how other people look at them.

We're all human beings; we get tired and we find things to be hard, especially when life gets to us. Managing your house with jobs like cooking, cleaning, paying the bills, being a personal driver to the kids, keeping the family schedule in control — and the list goes on — are on you, and it can be really overwhelming.

SAHMs can feel trapped. Being at home most of the time, being surrounded and followed by your kids and sticking to the routine at home makes you feel somewhat imprisoned, and you're left wishing for just a little time for yourself.

SAHMs also feel isolated. Not everyone relates to them, so almost all SAHMs create their own bubble with their kids, sticking to their comfort zones to feel protected and secure. They're living in their own world, so it could really give them hardcore anxiety once they have to come out of their bubble.

If you're reading the above statements and you are relating to it, I want you to know that you are being acknowledged; your value is important, and you are not alone in this, Momshie! However, I also want you to know that, despite hearing of the struggles and sad stories in the life of SAHMs, there are also some success stories too. And it's true that most of them also feel accomplished and happy.

Some Tips for Feeling Fulfilled as a SAHM

a. You are the boss, the queen. You're a badass! Nobody can tell you what you should and should not do. Your castle, your way. You make your own rules, and that alone is satisfying, bringing you a lot of joy and pride.

b. You are always present for a party! You heard me right, SAHMs. Go ahead and organize a lot of parties to celebrate every milestone of your children, or even of your husband. There's no greater joy than celebrating small victories together with your family and being able to witness all the milestones firsthand.

c. You are involved in your child's school performances. Having witnessed your children excel in what they do, whether it be in sports or academics, this is already going to make you a happy mom because yes, you did it, Momshie!

d. You're assured that your child is receiving the right amount of care and love from you. There's nothing more peaceful than knowing that your child is in the right hands and is safe because it's you and not anybody else looking after them and their wellbeing.

e. You create memories that are priceless. Memories are very important. You are always there, and you will always be part of your child's greatest memory. That's such a joy!

f. You will never be alone. Being at home means being with your family 24/7. There might be times that you need to be alone, but knowing that you can be with your family almost all of the time is a gift that is truly rewarding. It should never be taken for granted.

g. You're their teacher. It's so rewarding to see when our kids learn something good from us. Being with them most of the time will give you the opportunity to teach them, and to impart the wisdom and knowledge that only you can give.

If you've finally decided to take up the job and be a full-time mom, I want you to know that you're going to be successful. But let me share with you some tips to kickstart your new job

ACCEPT THE IMPERFECTIONS

You have to accept the fact that your house is not going to be clean all the time, and your kids will not behave the way you expect them to. Your life might be crazy sometimes, and you might not control everything that you want to, so you have to accept as early as now that all of these are okay; it is not your fault and will never will it be.

GO 🕉
MOMSHIE
LITTLE SECRET

You have to forgive yourself if things go to the left rather than to the right. All of us make mistakes and have regrets. You have to understand that some things are just not within your control, so you have to be kind to yourself and move forward one step at a time. You'll be much happier, and you'll be a better mom if you stop blaming yourself for things that have gone wrong. Keep reminding yourself of your intention — it matters.

KEEP YOUR COOL

Our children can be a handful sometimes, especially when we're around them for most of the time. So when they get to us, we lose our patience, we get angry, we get frustrated and we can become mean to them if we don't catch ourselves. You don't want to become a 'mean' Momshie, so learn to check in with yourself when you feel overwhelmed. Here are some techniques I use to keep my mind and emotions balanced:

The Power of Breathing

Don't underestimate the power that deliberate breathing gives you. It's a simple thing to do, yet we tend to forget to do it when we need it the most. If you're holding your baby or talking to your children, but they're refusing to listen, you lose your cool. You have to stop right there and take a deep breath for five seconds. You can even close your eyes, breathe in and open them again when you exhale. There's going to be a big difference in your approach towards your kids when you've done this. Give it a try!

Don't Overreact

If you're a reactive person, you might need to be very aware of those eruptive emotions that could surface to the top. Especially when you face something that you didn't expect or when you're in an unprecedented situation. Your children don't want to see a mom who's losing control amid problems; your children want to feel that you've got them when things get out of control. So chill out by putting things into perspective and focus on solutions rather than problems. A mom does not overreact when she chooses her words properly. Focus on what you can do, and focus on your words coming up in the most appropriate way possible towards your children. They learn from you, and a reactive parent will surely garner a reactive child. This is not rocket science, Momshies.

Go Back to Your Motivation

When you feel that you're irritated or upset with your children, get yourself together and go back to the question, "What motivates you?" More often than not, your motivation is your family or kids. By realizing your motivation, you'll have a shift of emotions. You'll understand that it's all about the well-being of your children, and not only just about what's good for you.

Learn Your Triggers

We all have our pet peeves, and knowing what those are in terms of parenting will be a great way to keep our cool; we can learn how to prevent them or ignore them when it happens. In this way, we are choosing our battles wisely. If we know them and are prepared, we're mostly able to surpass it and be cool for the entire day.

RELATE TO YOUR KIDS

Staying at home and doing things for our children can turn into a routine. All the errands, plans and activities can turn some of us into machines that are on autopilot. Therefore, it is so important to relate to or connect to your kids as early as their first months in order to learn how to bond and understand each other. You will see that when you listen to the signs from your young child, you will learn to sharpen your instincts as a mother. This will be helpful for when they get older and they need you for other circumstances. Keep the bond alive, Momshies, and let your child know that no matter what age they are, you are there for them.

How to relate or connect? Play with them, spend time with them. If you're running some errands, bring them with you. If you're cooking, teach them how to cook with you. Make things at home to create a learning activity for them. They'll surely love it, and it teaches them about responsibility as well. Even when your baby is very young, talk to them and coo with them. Speak to them like you would a good friend, so they will learn how to pick up the nuances of emotion from the tone of your voice.

EXTEND YOUR PATIENCE

When you become a parent, your patience will be tested over and over again. So right now, you've got to learn how to extend your patience and learn your limits. Patience is a talent because it can be   practiced by parents and it is THE key for surviving and soaring during your motherhood journey. You will need it for all ages of child, not just your little one.

GO
MOMSHIE
LITTLE SECRET

Finding Joy in Simple Things.

You have to learn how to be happy and jolly like a kid. Throw away your expectations and the feeling of entitlement. Focus on the present, and appreciate all the good little things in front of you. When you learn to smile because you had a warm delicious coffee in the morning, then you know that you're grounded and you rock at this job as a SAHM. Be grateful that you are able to stay at home and have the privilege of watching your child grow.

WORKSHEET FOR YOU TO PONDER UPON AND HELP YOU TO CREATE SOME SOLUTIONS

Write down your struggles as a SAHM

_____

_____

_____

_____

_____

_____

_____

_____

_____

_____

_____

Write down your joys as a SAHM

_____

_____

_____

_____

_____

_____

_____

_____

_____

_____

_____

_____

_____

_____

_____

_____

_____

_____

Share your favorite memory with your kids at home

_____

_____

_____

_____

_____

_____

_____

_____

_____

_____

_____

_____

_____

_____

_____

_____

What do you wish to change in your life?

_____

_____

_____

_____

_____

_____

_____

_____

_____

_____

_____

_____

_____

_____

_____

_____

_____

How do you feel most days?

_____

_____

_____

_____

_____

_____

_____

_____

_____

_____

_____

_____

_____

_____

_____

_____

_____

Share how you structure your day with your kids

_____

_____

_____

_____

_____

_____

_____

_____

_____

_____

_____

_____

_____

_____

_____

_____

_____

_____

_____

_____

_____

_____

_____

_____

_____

_____

_____

READ THE STATEMENT UNTIL YOU FEEL IT

I am a stay-at-home mom and my job is not easy. I shall ignore the people who look down on me and judge me because they're naïve. They don't know that our job is harder than they think. I am happy and content because I am loved by my kids and family. My job is so rewarding that no money can ever compete against it. I shall focus on the simple joys in my life and focus on what I can do. I shall forgive myself when things do not go according to the plan. I shall be confident and remind myself that I am a badass mom, and there's nothing I can't do.

_____

Signature & Date

CHAPTER 8

Keep the Fire Burning

The greatest question of them all: How can I be a great wife while being a supermom?

When I got pregnant with my little one, my husband and I decided to make an agreement that we should do whatever we could to maintain the romance between us, especially when the baby arrived. It's not uncommon to hear other people say things like, "Enjoy sex while it lasts because when you have a baby, it will be gone." Or, "Your priority will be your baby and not your husband." And even sometimes, "You and your baby are more important than your husband." The list goes on. As a young married couple and first time parents, we were alarmed to hear those horror statements that came from old married couples who had kids of their own. That's why we thought ahead and planned how to avoid those unromantic, dark days coming toward us. But sometimes, reality is stronger than our fantasy.

When I was recovering from childbirth, I had to admit that I *was* very focused on my baby and I. For the first couple of months, I found myself forgetting to give my husband good night kisses and good morning hugs, which I had loved doing before the baby arrived. I also felt that my sense of romance or intimacy had dropped. I don't know if it was the effect of childbirth or if I just suddenly had a change of heart. I'm certain that there was something happening within me, but I just couldn't understand it. I knew that dark days were coming, so I tried to shake those feelings off and tried to be intimate and romantic again with my husband. Some of the reason why the sudden shift in me occurred was because of my insecurity towards my postpartum body. Plus my preoccupied mind, full of baby stuff, was making it just too hard for me to focus on myself and my husband. I didn't know how to compartmentalize my mind and emotions, so I made myself believe that maybe this was just a phase of postpartum recovery, and I should give myself time and space to readjust.

Throughout the days, I thought I wanted to give up our agreement of keeping the romance alive and burning, but my husband remained consistent. He was there for me all the time to comfort me, to assist me, and to take me out when he saw that I was stressing out too much. He filled me with patience, understanding, support and love, and he mostly reassured me about myself.

He encouraged me and gave me time to go back to my fitness routine so that I'd feel confident again with myself.

I may have felt differently towards my husband had it not been for the fact that our communication remained unchanged. Just like our pre-baby life, I continued to talk to him about everything that I felt before I went to bed, especially when I felt shitty about myself. I didn't, and still don't, ever keep him in the dark, so he knew exactly what I was going through. I'm glad that he understood me and was proactive with it. With his consistent efforts and our great communication, we managed to get out of the tunnel together and reignite our romance. Now, I have a happy husband, and we rock parenting together with an even better mindset.

I may have been lucky to survive this challenge in our marriage, but we all know that, as time passes by, challenges will still come along when our family grows.

It's important to remember that motherhood can still be overwhelming and too demanding to leave energy and time for anything else. However, it's not a reason, and should never *be* a reason, to put your role as a wife on the backseat, Momshies.

I believe that some of us are failing with this because of the ongoing misconceptions of marriage after childbirth. If you see yourself making bold statements where you have to choose your baby over your marriage, then I want you to be fully aware of yourself, and try to act upon it deeply within your heart and mind:

My kids are my priority and nobody else.

This is true if you're a single mom, but this is a misconception if you're married. If you're living in a bubble, make sure to always include your husband. Remember, you made your kids together. He helped you to make them and he needs to help you to raise them. Let your husband be a part of your priority, and include him in everything you do. He deserves to be prioritized because, in return, he will do the same. Afterall, you and your kids are his priorities.

I'll just spend time with him later. I'm too tired right now!

Once you get used to saying this statement as an excuse for not spending time with your husband, it will soon become a habit. You will always think that he will understand that you are too tired because you took care of the kids for the whole day. Initially, I'm sure he will understand, but when your babies grow, he might want to spend some quality time with you.

He can't demand sex. I'm the one who gave birth, so I will just worry about it when I want to and maybe once our babies are a bit older.

The reality is that you might end up not having sex at all. Your husband might be patient enough to wait for you, but he might want to make love with you sooner than you might expect. He's not acting like a jerk if he asks for it; it's reasonable for a partner to engage with you intimately, especially when a few months have passed. You have to communicate with him and let him know when you're ready. If you're not, then don't be a cold wife by shrugging off his request all the time. Talk to him.

I've pushed myself hard so I can do everything for our kids, but what is he doing?

It is normal to feel like you are doing more than your husband when you are being a supermom. You might imagine that what he does is go to work and sleep throughout the night while you breastfeed your baby. Yet, your husband contributes to your family in his way too — you may just be overlooking his responsibilities. If you tell him that he's not doing enough, it might also frustrate him. So, you've got to stop demeaning your husband's effort, and try to appreciate even the small things that he does for you and your child.

I can live without his help because I'm a strong independent woman. I don't need him in my life to raise my child.

Being defensive is characteristic of a mother, especially when you feel that there's a predator coming. But your husband isn't the enemy here, so stop obsessing over this concept of always having to prove that you are a strong independent woman. You may want to change this statement when you're having a fight or disagreement with your husband. However, being alone shouldn't be an initial option to solve a fight. Separation is not doing anybody a favor. And yes, you can be a strong independent woman even if you have a husband, so you don't need to be alone to be called one.

These are only some of the misconceptions out there that won't help you to be a great wife. That's why it is important to realize that all of these come down to only one thing: your mindset. You have to set your mind to the things that matter; the things that help you to be a better version of yourself and to be a better wife or mom than yesterday. So if your mind is full of misconceptions like mentioned above, this is the right moment to delete, dump and burn it to the ground, ensuring that there's no way it will ever be in your head again.

But how can we really move forward with our marriage amid the pressure of being a good mom and being a great wife?

First of all, forget about the pressure and focus on your heart, Momshies. Communication is the key. This is NOT your first time reading this. We all know that constant communication is really the key to working out the dynamics in all relationships.

Make it a habit to communicate with your husband whenever you can. Don't leave anything unspoken. It could be some silly things you want to share with him, so you must go ahead and do this. Trust in the fact that he loves you, and he will listen to you. Give him the pleasure of knowing that he can be there for you as an individual as well.

But remember, communication is a two way process. Let your husband know that he can also communicate anything to you. When he feels that you're there to listen about his day, and you're ready to speak when he needs your reassurance and advice, he will truly understand how much you care about him.

So with communication being so important, here are some tips that you can do in order to be a great wife whilst being a supermom too.

Some practical ways to encourage constant communication

Go to bed at the same time: You can engage in your nightly conversations before going to sleep. It's the best time to talk about everything that's in your head because the house is quiet and dark. You may laugh together and even cry together. It's the best moment for cuddles too. I usually do this with my husband, and it's so funny how many things we actually can talk about before heading off to sleep. They have become our favorite moments together because it's just the two of us, and our hearts and ears are wide open for each other.

Eat your meals together: This may be difficult to achieve every day, but make sure that you have dinner together most nights if you can.

In my relationship, it's my husband who always waits for me in order for us to eat our dinner together. He likes company when eating because he believes that good communication happens over dinner as well. At mealtimes, you'll find yourselves talking about important things which make you both better partners for life.

Drive somewhere together: You can talk about a lot of things when you go for a drive. Once you're out of the house and in your car, you can also enjoy that moment and openly talk about your lives and your family in general. I do this almost every afternoon with my husband. Some days we just drive around our village whilst talking. It's a different venue, and we both find it really refreshing.

Treat him like your best friend and your partner in life: Becoming a mom made me a little bit scary and bossy at times. I want to say bitchy as well! You might agree that we often feel overwhelmed, and when this happens, we tend to take it all out on our husbands. Due to the challenges and shortcomings we face as a mother, we can slip into becoming a nagging monster to our husband. We have to stop doing that, Momshies. We have to stop blaming everything that goes wrong on our husbands. We have to learn to treat him as a partner in life; with respect and with love. If you're facing some troubles, talk to him calmly and you'll find that he'll be there to comfort you and to help you to face the challenges ahead of you. Let's make your marriage vow a reality. For better or for worse, you stick together!

Unlike us, fathers may not seem as natural when it comes to parenting. They can freak out faster and even feel lost for quite a while. That's why it's very important for us to take into consideration the feelings of our husband when it comes to parenting — it's his first time too.

I honestly thought at first that my husband was taking a back seat in parenting. However, he was actually freaking out because he wasn't sure what to do. So, I gave him some responsibilities and gradually included him in the routine of our child. By doing so, he learned how to parent our child with my help, and now we parent our child together.

Whatever situation you find yourself in, teach your partner to be a super dad. Throughout the process, you'll see that teaching him will bring you both even closer together — you'll bond through the experiences that you share together as parents. It will be fun and, one day, you will just find yourself laughing about some silly things your child has done.

Make love often: After giving birth, having sex is actually the last thing on our minds. Right, Momshie? This is totally fine because our body and minds need time to recover after such a long journey of pregnancy and childbirth. However, making love and being intimate with your partner is a part of your marriage, and it is something that you both should talk about and rekindle whenever possible.

It's true that you have to be ready before having sex again. However, you can still explore other ways to have fun and be intimate in bed without going through the whole process. What I'm trying to say is that whatever the case may be, you and your partner must make efforts to stay wild and hot for each other. Rejecting him without explanation might lead your relationship down a path where he finds other 'ways' to satisfy his needs. So, whenever you're ready, try to make sex a part of your life; it will help both of you relieve some stress, and you'll connect on a deeper and more intimate level.

Spend some proper quality time together: Being a mom gives us little to no time, but we have to schedule some date nights or even lunch dates, if possible, with our husband. It is important to spend a day out with our partner without the kids, once in a while.

Solve problems together: When we become a mom, we usually take all the responsibilities and burdens onto our shoulders when it comes to our kids. That's why we usually don't bother our husband with certain problems and challenges that come with motherhood. However, next time try to include your husband in solving some of the problems relating to your child, big or small. Working together and solving problems are what having a partner in life is all about. Dealing with problems as a couple, and being able to solve them together, will give you a sense of satisfaction and extra confidence and trust in your relationship. You're better when you're together, Momshies!

GO
MOMSHIE
LITTLE SECRET

I can write all the tips and romantic stories here, but the main takeaway that I want you to get from this chapter is 'choice'. It's just one little word, but it's a very powerful concept in any marriage. If you want to be a great wife while being a supermom, you have to make that choice every day. You have

to wake up in the morning and choose to love your husband unconditionally. Marriage is a lot of work, but it becomes manageable when you make your choices. Then you're set and ready, no matter what happens.

Remember, you got married because you chose him as your husband among all other men in this world. Always keep in mind that motherhood is a lifetime's blessing and a commitment. So you got this, Momshie! Keep rockin' the parenting world with the best partner you've got with you. Team work makes your love go wild. So keep the fires burning. Get it done!

Your Love Journal

In your mind, go down memory lane, and think about the most romantic memory you have of your husband. Write it down

_____

_____

_____

_____

_____

_____

_____

_____

Share your love story in a short paragraph to
remind yourself how you started a relationship

_____

_____

_____

_____

_____

_____

_____

_____

_____

_____

_____

_____

_____

_____

_____

_____

_____

What are the challenges you had, or are still having, in your relationship after you gave birth?

_____

_____

_____

_____

_____

_____

_____

_____

_____

_____

_____

_____

_____

_____

_____

_____

What are the changes you've noticed in your relationship since the baby has arrived? Good or bad, write it down now.

_____

_____

_____

_____

_____

_____

_____

_____

_____

_____

_____

_____

_____

_____

_____

_____

What are the things you love to do with your husband?

_____

_____

_____

_____

_____

_____

_____

_____

_____

_____

_____

_____

_____

_____

_____

Write down some ideas to reignite or spark the romance between you.

_____

_____

_____

_____

_____

_____

_____

_____

GO
MOMSHIE
LITTLE SECRET ACTIVITY

Write a heartfelt love letter to your partner, and put it in an envelope. If you're feeling creative, you can also design the envelope and attach some of your favorite pictures. When the letter and the envelope are ready, put it under your husband's pillow or on the breakfast table. Or maybe place it on the dinner plate before your partner sits down to eat.

In the letter, you may ask your partner to write back to you, just like the old days when writing a love letter was part of romantic life. You may start exchanging love letters for a week or a month. It's like a wonderful game that could really make you and your partner giggle, just like when you first met each other.

CHAPTER 9

Raising a Happy Baby

I never thought that our days would be filled with such joy and laughter caused by a tiny human being. His laughs and smiles literally make everybody giggle and shout for joy.

My inspiration, my sweet precious baby, Seiya, is such a happy baby. He always wakes up smiling at us, and he would gladly spend the day just laughing his ass off playing with us or playing with his toys. I often capture him, on my phone camera, making big smiles and laughing out loud, and I upload it on our page to share good vibes with everyone. People enjoy hearing him laugh, and they love him for it. Seiya's such a sunny boy!

People have asked me, "How do you manage to raise such a happy baby?" To be honest, it's not something that I've planned for, or thought deeply about. But having a happy baby in our home is something I and my husband always wished and hoped for.

However, upon thinking about the question, I started observing our practices at home to determine the things we do that make our little one happy. So, let me share with you, Momshies, our little hidden secrets to raise a happy baby. By adding or modifying a few habits to your daily routine, this can initiate joy and laughter in your home, which definitely transposes to your baby. Seiya is a true example of this.

Set Your Goal I remember the first time my husband held Seiya. He talked to him and said, "Hello, tiny human being. I want you to be a happy baby." From that day forward, we realized that our goal as parents was to make his happiness our goal.

The intention to create a loving and joyful environment for your little one has to be set as a priority in your mind and in your heart. Once you have decided to commit to that role, everything will just follow through, and you will realize you are doing the things unconsciously that will bring joy to your baby.

Also, creating a happy and healthy environment through relationships before your baby is born is very important; babies can feel everything in your womb, I promise you. I have witnessed anxious moms when they are pregnant, and when their babies are born, they end up being the same way. Mindset and emotions manifest the same way as physical ailments in an unborn baby. Happy Momshie pre-birth will surely create a happy baby post birth.

Talk happily with your baby I know it is hard to talk to a newborn because, more often than not, you will not be receiving any reaction from them. It is like talking to a wall, which actually discourages a lot of new parents to talk to their babies. However, it is important from the outset to talk to your baby about happy memories, fun little things and anything under the sun, really. Just keep on talking because, even if he or she does not react to it, your baby will definitely feel it. Your happy words and feelings are very important to your baby, so remember that.

I remember there was a time my husband and I were just talking about normal grownup things, but laughing about it whilst our son was around. You could see Seiya following our lips with his eyes, and once a while a little giggle popped out. We were the happiest parents alive when our baby suddenly reacted to our conversation, and this is such a remarkable feeling for new parents.

Acknowledge their emotions Saying simple words like, "I understand," or, "I get why you are crying," and, "I get why you are being fussy," will help you through the process of deeply understanding your baby's emotions. You may be thinking that your baby does not care if you validate his emotions or not, Momshies, but believe me when I say that babies are very smart. They know when you acknowledge their emotions by giving you a happy response.

Every time Seiya is crying and we figure out the cause of it, we always remind him that we understand how he feels and we give him some words of comfort to help him feel secure. This helps him to stop crying, and he listens instead and responds accordingly.

Remember, it is never too early to let your baby know that their feelings matter. Be there for them to celebrate victories, and especially when they are feeling down and crying. This is the time they are reaching out for more comfort than usual. Don't worry about spoiling them because this old adage is not true. So right now, throw that notion out and hug your baby just a little tighter when they need you the most.

Let your baby be surrounded by happy people
If you are living with your extended family, it is important to let them know your goal and to recognize the boundaries and standards that can sustain the happy environment you are about to create. In other words, it is important that other people, who are surrounding the baby, are on the same page as you. This means no family drama in front of the baby or any fighting or screaming. Any words or actions that don't bring happiness should be prohibited.

Every time my family is in front of Seiya, they always show their happiness by clapping their hands, singing songs and celebrating milestones while encouraging him to do new things. We can see that this method has a positive impact on Seiya because he automatically becomes more sociable, visibly enjoying the company of others.

Make sleep a priority Create a schedule for your baby's day naps and bedtime routine. It is really essential to adjust your schedule for your baby and not the other way around. Learn to recognize sleeping cues and gestures so you don't over-stimulate your baby. Babies need sleep, and when they get the sleep they require, they become a happy baby. It is like you, Momshie, when you lack sleep. You feel annoyed and frustrated. But a good night's sleep will help you to feel bright and sunny.

I make sure that Seiya has the right amount of sleep, and I think that this is one of the major reasons why he is such a happy baby. Since he is not yet a year old, he takes a nap twice a day for 1-2 hours per nap, and he sleeps 11-12 hours during the night. Keep in mind that sleeping schedules really depend on the age of the baby. If I were you, I would research more depending on your baby's age, so then you will have an idea of how much your baby should sleep. But it's true that all babies are unique — you should connect with your baby and understand when they are feeling drowsy and need to sleep. If you have a newborn, I suggest you always feed them on demand so your baby can prioritize sleep. Listen to your baby's cues as well.

Make playtime enjoyable This is the time and opportunity for your baby to be silly, to discover new things and to practice the things he has discovered himself. Make this a big part of your day. Make sure that it is enjoyable by setting him up with a lot of challenges, fun activities and musical experiences. You can also expose him to kids of his own age to make his or her playtime more interactive. Playtime is also the key to a good night's sleep.

We are the only ones playing with Seiya since we are living in unprecedented times. We always sit on the floor and play with him, imitate his moves and show him new possible ways to maximize his skills and capacity as a baby. We show him things like how to step using his feet correctly, how to clap his hands, how to do high fives or use some toys to stimulate simple learning. We noticed how much he learned when we allowed him to explore his own little world.

Give your baby your undivided attention Plenty of eye contact is necessary to connect with your baby as well as to set him up for happiness. When my husband is using his phone in front of him, Seiya will usually come and tap or yell to call for his attention. It is important to always show that you notice your baby and will always be there for them. This will make your baby feel secure and give them confidence to do everything they want to in the future.

When you are looking at your baby and connecting with him deeply, you will feel that it stimulates emotions that could result in the intellectual growth of your baby. Eye contact plays a huge part in the literacy and language development of a child.

We have now made it a habit to totally engage with Seiya. If we cannot give our one hundred percent undivided attention to him, then we make sure that someone else can in those moments. It is a fact that when a baby has attention deficit, it can make them grumpy and then they begin to act up all the time. This is a normal response because they are not getting the attention they deserve.

Respond to your baby when they cry It is really important to respond to your baby's cries, especially if they are newborns — it is their only form of communication to tell you that there is something wrong.

Of course, we let Seiya cry sometimes; it's part of being a baby. But when he cries, we let him know that we are there, and we respond to it by being curious. Such curiosity is an effective way to respond to our baby's tantrums. Honestly, Momshies; there will be times when we really don't know why our baby cries, but curiosity really helps parents to manage their own emotions while managing their baby's melt-down moments. Instead of telling your baby to stop crying, you should respond to them by asking why, and trying to work out what is going on. You can do a body check, and that's how you properly respond to your baby. So, it is not about giving in to your baby's demands all the time, but it is about understanding and preventing future undesired moments by picking up on his discomforts right away.

I notice that Seiya's cries differ depending on when he is tired, hungry or has a wet diaper. If you listen carefully and intuitively, you will begin to align with, and tune into, your baby's unique sounds. When you respond quickly to your baby's cries, you will notice that your baby will start to regulate his emotions properly, and he will be a happier baby.

Don't be too serious It is always good to add a little bit of fun to every moment and every challenge that you face in motherhood. Even though Seiya is a happy baby, of course he also has his moments. And sometimes we just imitate his crying or emotions in a fun way to try and divert his attention. This tends to result in him laughing, rather than crying, out loud.

I'm a big believer of laughter. In front of my baby, I am more than willing to make a fool of myself just to hear his loud laughter and giggle. And I love how easily my baby gets entertained. Just a simple and classic peek-a-boo will readily amuse him, but I know I have to find some other fun ways to entertain him as he grows older. But for now, I am content to be his clown and entertain him in simple ways.

When you make it a habit to have fun and take things less seriously, you'll notice that you're acting more relaxed as a mom. You won't sweat the small stuff, and you'll definitely embrace mistakes and imperfections with a lighter heart. If you're in a good mood and carrying an upbeat spirit, you'll eventually share it with your baby — that's how you raise a happy child.

CHAPTER 10

Common Mistakes of First Time Moms

Since baby Seiya will have become a one-year-old by the time I launch this book, I've realized some common mistakes that I have personally made in my first year as a first-time mom. I'd like to share them with you throughout this chapter.

Some of you might be able to relate to it, but sharing my experiences can help us to learn together. Either way, it's completely okay with me as I'm just being brutally honest with you, Momshies.

I think all of us make mistakes regardless of how long we have been a mom. However, it is important to note what we can do better after making those mistakes. My best piece of advice is to stop dwelling on our mistakes and to start learning from them in order to move forward as a great mom.

OOPS!!

Mistake #1
Listening too much to other people

I've mentioned in a previous chapter how other people have affected my parenting style and how much it has affected my peace of mind.

As a first-time mom, we usually experience getting unsolicited advice and, sometimes, it's helpful. But most of the time, it can lead us into a confused state of mind, especially when we start to believe everything we hear.

If I could go back in time to when I was still pregnant, I would listen less to other people and choose carefully what I believed in. This would have helped to make room for my own thoughts and decisions.

Having that sufficient amount of mental space for you to decide and formulate your own plans and thoughts is very important to personalize your own style in raising your child. Listening to the opinion of other people too much will not only affect you personally, but it will affect your child and their future too.

If you're in the same situation, start making your own decisions about what your baby is going to eat and wear that day. Those simple things will make you feel like you are in control. Believe it or not, even choosing the color and style of clothes for your baby may garner a reaction from other people which they may feel compelled to share. Peculiar? Not really. It's completely normal in this crazy, wonderful world called motherhood.

Mistake #2
Panicking over everything and over-thinking

I'm laughing my ass off while I'm writing this because I'm going to be forever guilty of worrying too much. My husband calls me a 'stress ball' because I always get nervous and panicky whenever there are changes happening with our little one.

For instance, whenever Seiya gets vaccinated, he always gets a little bit feverish, so I end up looking over him throughout the night and worrying about him through the day. Without my husband and my mom around, I would have probably rushed my baby to the hospital even with a slight fever. I'm so thankful for the support system who keep me in check and who assure me that all is well and good.

Aside from that, I always used to panic when Seiya got hurt when he was playing around in his crib. But later on, I realized that little bumps here and there were part of him exploring his skills and his limits as a little one.

Over this past year, I can say that I have learned to handle my emotions, and I've learned to distinguish between when to panic and when to stay calm. But if you ask my husband, Momshies, he would still say that I'm the most worried human being in the family. However, through research, learning to go with the flow and listening more deeply and intently to my intuition, I have learnt how to calm my nerves.

Mistake #3
Standing in the pee zone

I have a boy, and I'm sure you can imagine what happens whenever we're changing his diapers. It has happened so many times, especially during his newborn to infant stage. Now that he's a little bit older, I always notify him when I'm about to open his diapers, and I always have my burp cloth with me to serve as my shield if there's going to be a pee-splashing moment. Babies are just wonderful when it comes to surprises.

I have accepted that it's all part of caring for our baby, but I've learned that I can save my clothes from being pee-splashed by my little one through some preparation and by standing out of the 'pee splash zone' with a little bit of technique — I have mastered the art of standing at an angle when changing his diapers.

Mistake #4
Staying at home all the time

I'm the most fearful human alive. I was afraid to bring Seiya out of the house when he was born because of the pandemic happening in the world. On top of that, I was not confident enough as a first-time-mom to care for him outside our comfort zone. I felt like he was so fragile and I was so territorial; I would get upset or even scared when others would come and approach my baby or, even worse, try and touch him.

However, I knew that staying at home all the time was a mistake because it not only limited my baby's world and what he could see, but it also gave us the feeling of being stuck in one place, which was depressing and lonely.

It took me five months before I was ready to show him other things aside from what he could see in the house. We started going out into our backyard and strolling around the neighborhood. Recently, we even went to the beach.

Mistake #5
Putting too much pressure on myself

It was definitely a mistake wanting to be the perfect mom because there's no such thing. Social media is very good at showing ideal moms around the world, and it definitely dents my ego and pride as a mom every time I see somebody else doing a better job than me.

However, I've come to realize that putting pressure on myself will not give me anything good; instead it will just give me frustrations and other things to worry about, and that's the last thing we need as a mom. Trying to do everything like a superhuman is doable, but it's also torture for us, Momshies.

I've accepted the fact that there's certainly not enough of me to be the perfect mom, or to try and do everything myself. I have to ask for help. I have to be realistic, and I don't need to beat myself up. Neither do you, Momshie!

Mistake #6
Not bringing extra clothes

I'm not talking about an extra pair of clothes for my baby but rather for myself. Sometimes when we go out of the house, we tend to bring almost everything for our baby, but we forget about ourselves.

For instance, once we went to Seiya's check-up, and he suddenly threw up on me. It took me by surprise and I didn't have anything to cover myself up. I ended up looking and smelling like shit in public while carrying my little one around. However, I learned a very important lesson from that day forward — to bring extra clothes for myself, just in case any surprises occurred again when outside of the house. Just a reminder, Momshies, to think about yourselves as well!

Mistake #7
Buying too many expensive baby things and toys

As a first-time-mom, I guess it's normal to say that we just want to give the best to our little ones, and sometimes we over-indulge and end up over-spending on unnecessary items. This is a mistake because babies grow very fast, and their interest in things shift very quickly. Buying expensive toys or baby things can give you some heartache afterwards because you might just end up staring at it all in your storage room.

I've learned that I should only buy things that my baby can use for a couple of years; this way I am making sure that I have invested well for my baby.

CHAPTER 11

The Secret Weapon of a Great Mom

In our minds and hearts, we desire to be a great mom, but sometimes we need a weapon that can come in handy during trying times. In this chapter, I wish to share my own way of dealing with motherhood and some tips in general that might be used as your own secret weapon.

Riding this journey of motherhood for the first time made me numb sometimes. There were moments where I didn't know what to do and didn't know what to feel. It felt like I was learning my ABCs once again. A lot of people say that it's in a mother's nature to take care of her child; that I should never worry about it because it would come naturally. I partially agree with that. However, babies develop gradually, and they turn into tiny human beings who have their own personality and needs. As time goes on, we need to catch up to those changes.

To be honest, I'm always catching my breath. But there was a time when I stepped back and looked at my life from afar to see the bigger picture of the bubble I had created. I realized that I was being too paranoid, too rushed, too sensitive and too controlling. I knew that I had to change something in me; I knew that I had to be a better mom, not only for the sake of my child but also for the sake of myself. I made a shift and figured out that I had to bring my genuine self into motherhood.

I wanted my old self back — witty, determined, fun, authentic and organized — rather than the new paranoid, rushed, controlling and sensitive self-righteous woman that I had become. I knew that motherhood could be tiring, challenging and rewarding, but I never knew that it was such a powerful role that could overlap everything else in your life and could take over your identity. Please don't get me wrong, I love my identity as a mom, Momshies. It's the best blessing and the most prestigious role there is, but I also love who I was before I became a mom, so I didn't want to lose that. Instead, I wanted to combine them both to strive to be a better mom.

So I tried to look for some ways and some weapons out there by learning from other moms and reading some self-help books. It has actually helped me a lot. However, reading and learning are easy; the hardest part was when I had to turn all the lessons I learned into action. I can't tell you how much I did the trial and error strategy. It was like learning how to park the car — it needed practice, it needed to be at the right angle before moving, and it needed some resilience and patience to be able to park perfectly.

All right, so let's say that in doing the trial-and-error method, I tried to be a full-time mom as the first trial. This entailed doing everything for my baby, including the house chores and the only break I had was when I ate, went to the toilet and took a bath. No yaya, no helper. I did this for a couple of months and it got to me. It became one of the most difficult moments in my life. Nobody really warned me about the fourth trimester. Nobody warned me how, in fact, postpartum recovery and being a full-time mom could be so devastating and tiring. I tried to endure the exhaustion, the lack of sleep, the discomfort of recovery. I literally tried to eat and bathe like a soldier, just to get back to my baby fast enough to feed him and take care of him. I put my heart and my soul into the role; I was fully committed. I knew that being a full-time mom wouldn't be easy, and I thought I could do it all, but I realized that this was not the way I wanted to approach motherhood. I *could* do this, but this was not me. I had to remind myself that it was okay not to be happy doing this.

In the end, I had to scratch being a full-time mom off my list. And this is where I realized, and surrendered to, the fact that help is so important. Calling on people to give me some respite was what I needed in order to be a better mom with more patience; the mom I wanted to be.

Onto my next trial, in which I performed similar tasks, but this time around I took longer breaks and gave myself some free time to leave the house for a few hours a day. It was fun to be out of the house, to grab my favorite coffee and to spend time driving with my husband. However, I missed my baby so much that I realized going out didn't help me fully — I was still checking out the baby camera once in a while and was feeling mom guilt all the time. Thus, I ended up just rushing whatever I was doing, which in the end made me miserable because I wasn't fully engaging in anything (except in my paranoia about leaving my baby at home with a nanny).

Finally, I asked my mom to watch over my baby when I was away. At first, I began to feel guilty for leaving so many of my own motherhood responsibilities with her. I thought that it wasn't fair for my mom to take over, knowing how hard and tiring it was to take care of a newborn baby. But I also knew that I had to give myself some time away from my baby because I was beating myself up every day by being at home all the time. During these testing times, I hadn't yet mastered handling my emotions and my needs. Clearly, this trial didn't work out well because this made me more paranoid and I felt so guilty. So, I tried a third approach which required me to loosen up a little bit and take a breather once in a while. I started to accept help from other people. By going through the first and second trials, I discovered my weakness and strengths and the things that did and didn't work for me. That's why, in doing this third trial, I hoped there would be no more errors. I knew now exactly what I was supposed to do or change in my mindset in order to be a productive, happy and healthy parent.

The following steps that I'll be sharing with you are my own weapons in dealing with motherhood. I still call them 'steps' because I had to make that step or try to do it and, once I got the hang of it, then I felt that it was working.

The first step I made was to hire a yaya or a nanny. In chapter 1, I shared my process of hiring and training a yaya. It was thorough and quite strict because the life of my baby was at stake, and I had to be very meticulous in looking for the right person. This was a life changing decision I made, and I was happy that I did it. I had more free time to do the things I needed and loved to do, like running errands, cooking, exercise, napping and writing. I also noticed that I had more energy to play with my baby, which allowed me to become a better mom.

Since I work from home, I remained involved in my baby's routine. I still made his solid food, breastfed him and played with him. The only difference was that I was not stuck doing one thing only.

To be honest, it's not hard to take care of a baby, but it *is* hard to do something else while taking care of a baby. Now, I can do both things while feeling assured that my baby is receiving undivided attention and full time care from all of us. When everybody feels happy, the baby is even happier.

The second step was to schedule myself properly. I have mentioned the importance of scheduling in the previous chapters, and I just want to say that sometimes it's still a struggle for me to stick to it. But once I follow it through, I notice that life is so much more manageable.

I know for a fact that, as a mom, we all become so busy just thinking about all of our baby's needs and the things we have to do, and this makes our life so chaotic. That's why planning ahead or writing down a schedule can really help us to pull ourselves together. By doing so, I've managed to plan my baby's meals, our beach trips, writing this awesome book, keeping myself fit, designing our dream house and a lot more. Without my planner and notebook with me, I'd surely fail to attend to all the things I have to do because this Momshie brain can't take in a lot of things at once. I know you can relate.

The last step is to have plenty of sleep or take regular naps. At the moment, my baby can sleep 10–12 hours during the night, but he still wakes up once in a while for milk or for other reasons, like teething or stomach ache. So my husband and I always have interrupted sleep and end up feeling like zombies during the day. So taking a nap for at least an hour makes a world of difference.

Resting gives us the opportunity to rejuvenate and thus think clearly. Clarity is so important for mothers, Momshies, so don't skimp on your sleep. I've learned that there really is power in taking a 'power nap'. Sometimes, that's the only small thing I need for me to be able to function well throughout the day. It gives me the energy and the peace of mind to continue on with my day. It clears my head and helps me to think, to make wise decisions or even to write better. I can't tell you how much sleep I lack, but I can tell you how much sleep we need as first-time-moms, Momshies (maybe seven hours of sleep during the night and an hour's nap during the day would be amazing). Whenever I feel sleepy, I take the opportunity to tuck myself into bed and sleep.

These are my top three steps that turned into my little secret weapons in dealing with this crazy yet enchanting world of motherhood. These are things that make me strong and that make me a better mom. This may or may not work for you; what matters is that you know how to pick your weapons depending on what *does* work for you. Your way, your own secret weapons.

As time passes by, and as your baby grows, you will discover some other things that can help you along the way, so here's a bit of advice: don't resist change — embrace it and deal with it.

Other than the weapons I've shared with you personally, here are some of the other secret weapons that can probably help you become a great mom:

a. A secret weapon does not have to be a thing. It can also be a person such as your husband or partner. Being your secret weapon means that they are helping you to be a great mom by sharing the responsibility with you full time. For example, when you're working, or when they are helping around the house so you can take a nap, or when you are engaged in other tasks that require your undivided attention away from your baby. It may sound cheesy, but our partners can really make this journey more fun, and they can help to lighten the load. Knowing that somebody is there for us, who is ready to back us up when times get tough, can easily ease the worry in our mind and heart.

    This secret weapon could also be our mom or any member of the family. Transitioning into motherhood becomes easy when our 'somebody' from the family has decided to stay with us for a couple of weeks until we have recovered from the birth. I'm lucky enough to have a mom who's nearby and who was willing to help me transition to this role of motherhood. I can say that she was my secret weapon in the first weeks after giving birth, and her presence alone just made everything manageable and tolerable.

b. Quiet time to listen to trendy music or a podcast. Many of us experience being stuck in a loop of children's songs and stories in our minds. So whatever opportunity you get to hear some grown-up music, or smart conversations on a podcast, will help to jumpstart you even while you are running errands or just going to the supermarket.

Do this a couple of times and you will recharge and make yourself feel involved and reconnected to the world outside of motherhood. Listening to music while driving is also such a great way to feel liberated, and it helps to ease your mind. Music can be such sweet surrender without you even noticing the impact it has on your overall psyche. So pump up the music, Momshie, and revel in the beat and harmony of your life.

c. Going to the beach or being close to nature often could also be one of your secret weapons. People surround themselves all the time in nature to unwind and to think. For moms also, we go for the same reasons — to walk, to sit, to swim, to play with our kids, to relax, to run and, most importantly, to feel happy.

My family would choose to get away every month and go to the beach to get a dose of Vitamin Sea, if possible; to feel the freedom and power to do whatever we want to do and be whatever we want to be. Also, there's a magical power which belongs to the beach, so when we return home, we all feel a little calmer, more relaxed, more grateful and a little more centered.

I was writing this book during the COVID-19 pandemic when there were different regulations in each part of the country and throughout the whole world in general. However, we still managed to go to the beach — a remarkable experience that brought my whole family relaxation through a deep connection with nature and with life.

d. Sleep training. Moms who are able to sleep train their baby as early as six months can finally enjoy the leisure of sleeping through the night. Most of these moms say that it is their favorite secret weapon, as it brings them a lot of freedom during the night.

Sleep training may not work for all babies, but it can for some. For your baby to be able to sleep through the night without interruption is the most prayed for situation regarding all mothers in the universe. It's a win-win situation for you and your baby. So, congratulations if you're one of the lucky ones, Momshie!

e. Coffee. Who does not need a coffee? All moms need that caffeine kick to be able to start the morning right, especially if you're still lacking some sleep because of the baby waking up during the night.

Drinking coffee gives you time to relax for a little while and think about the day you're about to face. Coffee helps me, personally, to be a great mom because it gives me more energy. Some people may choose to drink tea. Whatever gives you that small boost in the morning, make sure you take the time to savor it as you begin your day.

f. Baby Carrier. Everything can be a secret weapon, including the one thing you use ninety percent of the time — your baby carrier.

Some babies just want to be carried all of the time, and moms have suffered from backaches and arm aches. Thank goodness for wonderful baby carriers. They save us from any aches and pains, and they also make our hands free, giving us the opportunity to do other things like house chores or typing on the computer while carrying our little ones.

For instance, my own baby boy, Seiya, does not want to be put down during his day naps, and the only thing that helps me to get through this challenge is a nice quality baby carrier and loads of patience. It can be a tough challenge, but I'm always up for it because I have a secret weapon with me.

The list of secret weapons goes on, but always remember that you'll have your own weapon that you will discover and that will work marvelously in your life.

How about you, Momshie? What are your secret weapons?

_____

_____

_____

_____

_____

_____

_____

_____

_____

_____

_____

_____

_____

_____

_____

_____

SPECIAL CHAPTER

Our COVID19 Story

While writing this book, my baby boy and I contracted the coronavirus and, if you're following us on my Gomomshie.com Facebook page or my personal Instagram account, you will see how our journey through this ordeal panned out. I've allotted the last pages of my book to talk about my excruciating experience and my thoughts during and after our self-quarantine at home. I hope that I'll be able to create awareness that will serve as an inspiration to all of you.

In this chapter, I'll be writing my thoughts from two different perspectives: as a mom and as an individual. But before we start to dig deeper into my realizations, let me tell you what really happened and how we contracted the virus.

I had thought that we were careful and I had thought we were being safe. At this point in the book, it had been a year since the quarantine had started in the Philippines but still, each day, I worried for the safety of my little one. Apparently, worrying and compliance with safety and health protocols were not enough. The virus just hit you when you least expected it. I can't express it enough when I say that this virus did not spare anyone. Nobody was exempt.

One afternoon, we decided to do more than just wave to our neighbors over the fence. My little one, together with my 63-

year old mom, my 6-year old nephew and Yaya, went around the neighborhood for an afternoon stroll. Since there had been a pandemic for a year, my baby and nephew needed to get out of the house, even for thirty minutes, and they strolled nearby to get some fresh air and sunlight (we don't have a big garden to stroll around). It had become our new routine, and our neighborhood seemed to be safe because the village admin usually notified us of the areas which had COVID cases. At that time, nobody along our street had any symptoms or had contracted the disease; well, at least that's what we thought.

I remain sure that my baby and Yaya contracted the virus from that stroll because that was also the day when Yaya first felt sick. That was also the day that we found out from a friend that there were positive cases around the neighborhood.

Yaya went home for her day off. When she returned, she told us that although she had a fever, she wasn't worried because she said it could be her UTI. She reassured us that she already felt okay, and that was why she had decided to show up for work. I didn't worry because I thought that she had gone to the hospital and been diagnosed with the UTI. I trusted her.

However, the day that she returned to us, I started feeling tired and was having muscle pains. Seiya also started to be fussy, especially during his mealtime. He was usually such a happy eater, and he usually finished his food, but I noticed that since Yaya had returned to us, his appetite had changed — he was failing to finish the food that we prepared for him. After that day, I still continued doing my usual routine until one night I had a fever and chills. I thought it was mastitis since my breasts were also sore. I took a paracetamol and tried to sleep it out.

However, my fever did not go away for two days, and that's when I decided to call a swab team to check on me. The thing that I was most afraid of happened; I tested positive, and what's worse is that my little Seiya also tested positive. Yaya tested positive and, on that day, she was also still running a fever. The rest of my family members who were staying with us had to start on home quarantine too, for a seven day incubation period. On the sixth day, my six-year-old nephew showed symptoms, and unfortunately, he tested positive for COVID too. All the family members had to do a re-swab.

My husband, who had been in close contact with me and Seiya, amazingly turned out negative for COVID, and that's something I'm so thankful for. My senior citizen mom, who had also been on the afternoon stroll that fateful day, luckily did not get infected. It was a very emotional and challenging time for all of us. The rest of the family was very stressed out because of our situation, and they were fearful that they might also become infected.

There was no need to blame anyone for bringing the virus into our house, but it became clear how important contact tracing was in order to give proper information to the people around you so to contain the virus.

I began to journal and document my thoughts, as well as my mental and physical well-being, and I'd like to share these with you now, Momshies.

DAY 1
POSITIVE VICTIMS OF COVID
MOMMY AND SEIYA

The moment that I knew I tested positive, I couldn't help but cry out in fear. The doctor who did the swab test did a very good job in calming me down. They explained the things I should expect and do in order to recover. However, when I knew that my baby was positive too, my heart just suddenly dropped, and my tears fell like waterfalls. I was blaming myself for not being able to protect him and for not keeping him safe. He was such an innocent little boy, so how could this world punish him with a deadly virus? My thoughts were racing around my head like a wild beast. I felt depressed and hopeless.

The first day was tough, and the first night in quarantine was the hardest. I was in shock, and it was very hard to process everything that was happening around me. I wouldn't worry and focus on myself because my little one was my priority. I was so afraid that something might happen to him that I couldn't even sleep a wink during the night.

The fear was eating me alive during the first day, and it is important to emphasize that here. The news on TV and in online articles continuously focused on the intense and worst effects of COVID-19, and this played a big part in creating fear in society, and in me. I was so scared when I tested positive because I saw on TV how scary it could be. My mind started to flashback to the articles online that I had read, and I remembered the pictures I'd seen on the news or on social media. I started to panic and over-think things. After that night, and over-thinking to the point of exhaustion, I realized that I wasn't going to recover in a timely manner if I didn't shift my mindset.

My sister, who's a registered nurse, reassured me that everything was going to be okay as long as we took the prescribed medicines to treat the symptoms. We had to follow healthy guidelines so we could recover faster. She explained to me the statistics of those who had recovered from COVID within my age group, and she did the same for my baby. This continuously affirmed to me that we could fight off the virus in no time.

My husband even said that although the virus was no joke, there was really no need to panic. Upon hearing all of their advice, my mind suddenly shifted from hopelessness into a mindset of a wild mother lion, who was ready to do whatever it took to save her little one.

IN THE MIDDLE OF QUARANTINE

After a couple of days in quarantine, more symptoms started to manifest. It began with a cold, a sore throat, heavy chest, conjunctivitis and, on top of all that, I then lost my sense of smell and taste. Though my fever was gone, my other symptoms were getting stronger, and I felt weaker each day. I thought I was not progressing, and my medicines were not helping me.

Meanwhile, my little one had few symptoms. He randomly sneezed and coughed, but he didn't have a fever, and his appetite was back to normal. He was such a happy eater and a ball of energy throughout the entire quarantine period. It was such a relief for me to see him happy and with his normal energy, despite the virus.

REALIZATIONS

AS A MOM IN QUARANTINE

My little one was eleven months old when I wrote this, and before the quarantine period, he had never been sick (except for a slight fever after being vaccinated by his pediatrician). So when this virus hit us, I was sick to my stomach because I couldn't bear the thought of Seiya being infected and having to experience symptoms that we might not have been able to handle.

However, as moms, we tend to keep our worries to ourselves, and we keep moving forward. It's like an automatic setting in our heads to set aside our emotions in order to focus on our babies' needs and health.

So, instead of showing Seiya that I was sick or feeling weak, I tried to act strong and happy in front of him, continuing with our usual daytime and bedtime routines. It also somehow helped to divert my own feelings from sorrow to happiness.

I've come to realize that when we become a mom, and even though we're sick, our love and care for our baby is always our main priority. It's amazing how I managed to care for him when I was sick. Looking back, it almost seems impossible, but somehow I mustered up the drive and energy that switched on when my baby needed me and when we were in the most difficult time of our life. It was like an electricity generator that worked when the lights were shut off.

But I have to be honest with all of you, Momshies. It was difficult at times to look after him when I was debilitated and sick. Let me share with you a specific night when I almost lost my sanity.

Imagine yourself being locked up in a room with your little one, all day and all night long, for two weeks. There was one night that Seiya did not let me sleep for the entire night. He kept waking up and wanting to be swayed. However, my weak body would not physically let me sway him. I just couldn't lift him up. It was hopeless, and I couldn't ask anybody to help me because we were in quarantine.

I let him cry for a couple of minutes, but his incessant crying was eating at me, making me want to scream. I thought I was going to lose my sanity. I started to raise my voice because I was running out of patience, and I was running out of ideas as to how I could stop him from crying. I wanted to sleep and rest, but I couldn't.

Finally, at six in the morning, I was feeling like a mad zombie. I turned on the lights and opened the door. When my husband showed up in front of me, I couldn't help but cry out and rant while in tears. I was breaking down, literally. I felt like I had lost myself, and I was going crazy. I was desperate; I couldn't even hug my husband or lean on his shoulders like I used to do whenever I was in distress. It was one hell of a night.

I now realize that it was not entirely because of Seiya's acting up for the entire night that caused me to react, but also the isolation of having to do everything on my own with no help or support around me. It was a challenge. Now that we are out of quarantine, and everyone is home again, I am so grateful for all of the help and support that is around me. I have gained a new appreciation for the word 'help'.

Being in quarantine with my little one tested our relationship and the length of patience I could extend to him. It was a big stretch for us. It was hard, and for sure it was an adjustment for Seiya too, but I'm glad that, at the end of the quarantine, we both grew and stepped up our relationship to a different level. We became closer, like best buddies.

AS AN INDIVIDUAL IN QUARANTINE

I thought that being infected by this virus would be the end of me. Every night when I lay in bed, I was afraid that I wouldn't be able to breathe again. I was afraid to close my eyes knowing that I might never see the light ever again. My heart was racing all of the time.

This was me. These were the feelings running deep inside of me. It got worse, especially when my symptoms increased and my fear and anxiety escalated. Sometimes, I had a mild panic attack which affected my breathing. It was frightening, but I figured out how to handle my nerves and to stop myself from being paranoid.

I realized at the time the importance of mental health. It's true that being isolated can lead to depression, and it makes you think of the worst things that could happen; that's really horrifying. However, it's normal to be in this state of mind, but keeping those negative thoughts in your mind each day will undoubtedly bring you down.

One of the secrets to recovery is your mind — mind over matter. As an individual who was infected by COVID-19, my mind became my shield, protecting me from all the symptoms and pains I experienced. It was my armor that kept me ready to face my battles each day.

I was able to manage my mind by filling it with positive thoughts and focusing on the love and care of the people around me. It wasn't easy to look at the brighter side of the situation, but I knew in my heart that it was necessary in order to survive and to stay strong amid the heavy storm I was in.

I also realized that it's important to truly accept the fact that nobody can help you but yourself, especially when you're dealing with your own way of thinking. Yes, there are people around you who have your back, but it's important to truly understand that the real power of healing is within you. Only you can make yourself get out of bed each day.

Another little secret that I want to share with you is my faith, Momshies. During desperate times, it's normal that we rely on God, Buddha, Allah and other super beings to help us to stay strong. I believe that it helps, and I believe that prayer works. It also gives us comfort and the hope to recover and to witness another sun rise in our lives. That's one of the things I did, and it helped me to sleep at night. It helped me to believe that there's somebody out there who's listening to me and my prayers and who is guiding me.

Faith is the glue that binds our hearts and thoughts together. Prayer is a powerful tool, Momshies. Even if you're not religious, try thinking of yourself as a superpower; a divine being who can overcome any obstacle.

I've fought so many battles in my life, but this one was the scariest and the most unexpected one. When things are unexpected, it either it gives you joy or it puts you in danger.

POST-RECOVERY THOUGHTS
Seiya and I tested negative after two weeks in self quarantine,

and it brought so much joy to the whole family. My husband literally jumped up and cried with tears of relief, and I had never seen him like that before. It was like we had won the race and we finally had achieved victory.

I was so relieved when my body was finally free of the symptoms and when I slowly felt my energy coming back again. It made me realize how much I took my life for granted. Since then, I have made a pact with myself to consistently appreciate my life and to invest in my health, myself, and my child.

The excruciating experience that I had with my little one was an eye opener for everyone, and it was a lesson to us all to prioritize health and to treat COVID-19 seriously. Even though we survived the virus, the bigger, global battle is not yet over as I sit here and write this. There's still a surge of cases in the Philippines each day and, to be honest, now I've had the experience of being infected by the coronavirus, I am more scared of it than ever.

The whole family has increased health measures at home, such as increasing the intake of vitamins in order to improve our immune system. Everybody understands the severity of the situation, but together we're learning to live like armies; strong and ready to face the storm. I hope you are too, Momshies.

GO MOMSHIE
FINAL LITTLE SECRET

There's one important thing that I want to share with all of you, and I want you to keep this in mind for as long as you need it, especially when things are getting out of hand. I may have kept this from all of you for quite some time, Momshies, but I am now ready to reveal it and share it with you here. There's only one thing that you might need in order to live happily as a mom, and that is perspective.

Perspective? What is it anyway? It is simply the way you look at things. In our case, it's simply the way you see motherhood. You may not realize it now, but there's power in perspective.

It is so powerful that it can make or mark your life as a mom, so it's important to understand how your perspective works and how it can help you to become a better mom. In this motherhood life, there are things that are clearly right and wrong. What we usually have are two perspectives on one thing.

A good example is breastfeeding. We have one mom who says that it is difficult, and there's another mom who says that 'difficult' is an exaggerated word to use when describing breastfeeding. Moms can either continue arguing and maintaining their idea about breastfeeding, or they can begin to value the differences in others and learn to accept other people's opinions. That is perspective.

It is important to note that your perspective on motherhood determines how you handle relationships with your family — how you deal with challenges and troubles and how you will decide to live your everyday life as a mom. You may not realize how important perspective is until you realize that it is all in your hands. Moreover, your perspective affects everybody around you.

If you have a bad or negative perspective on motherhood, you will find yourself constantly yelling at your kids, getting overly exhausted, hating your situation and not being able to accept the requests of your kids.

More often than not, as a mom, we often over-think and stress ourselves out with simple things that simply require a shift in our perspective. A good example may be when your kid has been silly the whole day and he accidentally drops and breaks a glass. Due to your annoyance and exhaustion, you might blow up and blame it on your kid for not listening and following your instructions or warnings all day long. You may get frustrated over what happened and become a grumpy mom.

However, if you could only shift your perspective, you might realize that what happened is a safety threat, and that your initial reaction should be to check on your kid and make sure that he's okay and nobody got hurt. You may feel relief that your kid is safe, and it's just a glass that's broken. Then you begin to feel grateful that your child wasn't hurt, and you shift from worrying about the broken glass to the well-being of your child. That's a shift in perspective.

If you have a good perspective on motherhood, you find yourself open to seeing other moms' perspectives that could nurture relationships in your own life. You have a lot of reasons to be grateful and happy despite troubles or shortcomings in your life. If you continue living with a good perspective, you'll become not just a better mom, but a happy mom.

Another good example is when you see the stretch marks on your body. Or maybe when you consider the pregnancy fat that hasn't left your body; it's taking its time and sitting there for too long. You may hate it and shame your body because of pregnancy, but if you shift your perspective in a good way, you'll realize how amazing your body has been for the past 9 months of pregnancy. And then it gave birth to a tiny human being who gives you the most satisfaction and happiness in the world. You'll find yourself loving your body even more despite the changes, and you'll feel proud when you see your stretch marks and you'll call them 'warrior marks' as a reminder of how you survived pregnancy and childbirth. That's a shift of perspective and it feels amazing!

Let me tell you this, right here, right now. Shifting your perspective is an everyday battle; it's not an easy task to always look at things on the brighter side, especially when life throws us a curveball. But let me remind you, Momshies, that each problem is an opportunity to grow. This is how you should see the battles in your life as a mom.

You might say that I am living in a fantasy world if I dare you to keep a good perspective on motherhood all of the time, but let me be frank when I say that nobody's telling you to shift overnight. It is indeed a process, and it will take time. As long as you practice or train yourself to always have a good perspective on motherhood, you will do just fine.

So let me share with you some of the things you can do in order to have a good perspective.

Stop complaining. I have already lost count of how many times I have complained since becoming a mom. There were moments that I just whined over simple things. As a mom, we love to complain how things are not going our way and how other people are not being sensitive enough towards our situation. If you let me continue, the list of things that moms can complain about is endless. So, let's break that habit, Momshies. Let's stop complaining and talk instead about our joys. That's how you can shift your perspective.

Stop arguing on social media. All of us are entitled to post on social media, or on mom groups that we're a part of, and it's inevitable that moms talk about some sensitive motherhood issues and concerns that trigger debates and arguments. There are going to be a lot of opinions, and others might disagree with you. Responding to negative posts with maturity and lightheartedness will lessen any bitter criticism and instead build healthy conversations.

When you are browsing on social media and reading some trigger comments on your posts, always remember to find the angle of the one disagreeing with you. You should also understand that your opinion is not fixed and can be changed, so letting somebody else's ideas into your head won't be an attack on you. If someone wants to let you know that your opinion is wrong, look at it as an opportunity to boost your creativity and even offer some of your own solutions about what's being discussed.

If you find that social media has become toxic, and it's not helping you to create a positive outlook on motherhood, you may want to undergo a social media detox for a while — that really does help.

Start seeking happiness. If you keep on looking for happiness, you'll find yourself feeling grateful, always smiling and often laughing. During trying times, you may want to stop for a little while and look around you. You may find something that makes you happy, like the painting on the wall, your family pictures or just your favorite mug on the table. Notice them, especially when things are getting tough. Having them in your life, and keeping those happy memories and feelings with you will definitely help you to keep a good perspective on motherhood or even on life in general.

Start talking positively. You may want to start exploring positive vocabulary and practice using it in your everyday life. A big difference occurs when you learn how to say,

"You are beautiful."

"You are gorgeous."

"You have a wonderful smile."

"Your voice lights up my heart."

Say these positive words to other people as well as to yourself... You will find yourself bringing positivity all around you through your words.

You might think that words are just words, but I want you to realize that words are such powerful things that can build perspective, develop character and change the world.

When you realize the importance of your perspective, I want you to always think before you yell, and close your eyes before you get frustrated. Think about your viewpoint on motherhood, and make sure to always go back to what makes you happy and what works for you as a mom.

I may have given you a lot of tips and suggestions to help you get through the early months and years of motherhood, but what I want you to do now is to deeply connect and discover that the power of your actions has the ability to impact your state of mind. Those actions will also impact those around you.

Perspective is key, and being able to flow with new discoveries will surely open up a whole new world of motherhood for you. Enjoy the ride because there is no other day than today. Have fun and **GO MOMSHIE**!

"I never knew I could love two men in my life."

-Victoria Dang

www.ingramcontent.com/pod-product-compliance
Lightning Source LLC
LaVergne TN
LVHW011156080426
835508LV00007B/445